20 STEPS TO BETTER SOCCER

Dan Woog

ROXBURY PARK

LOWELL HOUSE JUVENILE

LOS ANGELES

NTC/Contemporary Publishing Group

Published by Lowell House
A division of NTC/Contemporary Publishing Group, Inc.
4255 West Touhy Avenue, Lincolnwood (Chicago), Illinois 60712-1975 U.S.A.

Lowell House books can be purchased at special discounts when ordered in bulk for premiums and special sales. Contact Department CS at the following address:
NTC/Contemporary Publishing Group
4255 West Touhy Avenue
Lincolnwood, IL 60712-1975
1-800-323-4900

ISBN: 0-7373-0467-7
Library of Congress Control Number: 00-132028

Roxbury Park is a division of NTC/Contemporary Publishing Group, Inc.

Managing Director and Publisher: Jack Artenstein
Editor in Chief, Roxbury Park Books: Michael Artenstein
Director of Publishing Services: Rena Copperman
Editorial Assistant: Nicole Monastirsky
Interior Design: Carolyn Wendt
Interior Illustrations: John E. Kaufmann
Cover Design: Kristi Mathias

Printed and bound in the United States of America
00 01 02 DHD 10 9 8 7 6 5 4 3 2 1

Contents

1 Ball Control Basics

Yikes! Sometimes it seems as if balls are flying at you from all directions. High, lofted kicks seem to drop from the sky; line drives carom off the crossbar; miskicks from the other team take crazy bounces; and, of course, teammates slam the ball at you, then expect you to control it even at your foot or chest.

Can you handle all those soccer balls?

Sure!

How can you do it?

Practice!

One of the most important parts of soccer—it might even be the key to the whole game!—is feeling comfortable with the ball. That means no matter what direction it comes from, at whatever speed, and whichever part of your body you use, you feel confident you can control the ball.

That's right: *You control the soccer ball. It does not control you.*

You want to develop enough confidence to stop the ball with any part of your foot: bottom, inside, laces (or instep), even the outside! You want to be able to take the ball out of the air by making a "tabletop" with your thigh.

You want to control a chest-high ball by arching back, then letting it drop to your feet. And you definitely want to feel that your head and the soccer ball are good friends, not mortal enemies.

Foot

Let's start with the feet, since that's the body part you'll use most for control. (If your teammates haven't gotten into the habit of passing the ball to your feet, it's time they learned!)

Although the foot is both versatile and flexible, the two most common areas used to master control are the soles and insides. The sole of the foot is used most often to stop the ball dead (although you can then add a quick little flick with the bottom of the foot to move the ball in the direction you want it to go). To control the ball with the sole of the foot, lift it slightly as the ball approaches. If you lift it too high, the ball will skitter on through. With the heel locked and the toes pointing slightly upward, bring the foot down until it gently meets the ball. Make sure you're touching the ball with the front part of the foot—if you use the middle part of your foot, or the heel, you

have very little control. (It's important to "feel" the ball, and you can't do that with the thicker parts of the bottom of your foot.)

You use the inside of your foot to control the ball, but keep it moving. As the ball comes toward you, lock the ankle. When the ball is near, bring the foot slightly back, to cushion the impact. (Think about catching a baseball with your hand. You wouldn't stick your glove out and let the ball go SMACK! into you, would you? It's the same with soccer. "Give" a little as the ball strikes your foot.) If you keep your foot pointed the same way on impact, the ball will roll in the direction from which it came. If you turn your foot slightly, the ball will roll the opposite way. It all depends which way you want to "play" the ball. The key is to keep the ball within "playing distance"—no more than a step or two away from you.

Using the outside of the foot is a bit trickier. You use this type of control to keep the ball away from an opponent who is close to you. As the ball comes near, roll your ankle to the outside. Make a scooping motion with your foot, and push the ball the direction you want it to go. Be careful not to do this too sharply, or the ball will bounce away or go over your foot.

Sometimes you'll use the top of your foot (the laces) to control a bouncing ball. Depending on the height of the bounce, you'll either extend your foot straight out (with a flat surface), or point your toes slightly upward. Either way, make sure your foot is one or two inches off the ground. As the ball hits the top of your foot, "give" a little (as before, think about catching a baseball). Some players cradle the ball on the top of the foot; others flick it off to the side.

Thigh

After the feet, the next most common body part used to control the ball is the thigh. (This only works for balls in the air, of course!) As the ball nears you, raise your leg so that your thigh forms a "platform." When the ball hits your thigh, give a little (remember baseball?). From there, the ball should drop to the ground; then you can play it. With practice, you'll be able to move the ball from one thigh to the other before letting it drop.

Chest

Experienced players can even use their chests to control a high ball. As it comes out of the air, arch your back; your hands should be held up next to your chest, for balance. Lean back; let the ball touch your chest, then let it drop to the ground. When you feel comfortable, you can give a little twist with your upper body when the ball hits; this turns the ball in the direction you want.

2 Ball Control Exercises

Figure Eights

One of the easiest ways to feel comfortable with the ball is by practicing "figure eights." This works as follows: Take a ball and—using the bottoms, insides, and outsides of one foot—move it in a figure-eight motion around the other foot. At first you will go slowly, feel awkward, and occasionally even stop. Soon, however, the ball will glide along in a familiar pattern; you'll move it quickly, and without stopping. When you can do that, try to do it without looking at the ball.

Tossing It Up

You can practice control by yourself, or with a partner.

If you're alone, throw the ball into the air. After it bounces, control it with the various parts of the foot. Before it bounces, work on control with your thigh or chest.

If there is a kickboard nearby, great. If not, any sturdy— *very* sturdy—surface, like the side of a building, will do. (We don't recommend garage doors. And if all you've got is a brick or concrete surface, use an old ball—it scruffs up pretty quickly.) As the ball rebounds to you, practice controlling it with different parts of the foot. Don't be satisfied with stopping it dead; use your first touch to position it in the direction you want to move.

A friend, neighbor, sibling, or parent can also toss you some balls to help you improve your level of control. These can be high balls and low ones; balls kicked right at you; and some for which you must move. Try to use the most appropriate form of control for each particular situation. It's not something you can figure out ahead of time; the idea is to make the decision (sole of the foot or inside? thigh or chest?) based on the direction and speed of the ball.

If you've got several friends or teammates, ask them to form a circle around you. They will feed you balls to control—slowly at first, then in a more rapid-fire manner. In the beginning, they should feed you in a preplanned rotation, either clockwise or counterclockwise. As you get better, the feeds should be random (it helps if they yell your name a second before they serve). Now you've got to react quickly, and position your body properly.

With time, start trying to add more than one touch. In other words, control the ball first with one thigh, then the other, before letting it touch the ground. Or try for a chest/thigh/top-of-the-foot combination. Make up your own series, too.

With friends, you can also play a fun game called . . .

Zelmo

Zelmo is similar to the basketball game Horse, except (duh) you've got a soccer ball, you can't use your hands, and you're spelling a different word. And, oh yeah, you're juggling soccer balls instead of shooting basketballs.

Players form a circle, and try to keep the ball in the air as long as they can. You are allowed to use any part of your body except your hands. If you can't control the ball, or your pass goes way outside the circle, you get a *Z*. The first player to spell the word *Zelmo* loses, and sits down. The game continues until a winner emerges.

Beginners can start by tossing the ball with their hands, and can let the ball bounce once between each juggle if they have to. Intermediate players should start by flicking the ball up with their feet, and should not let the ball bounce. Experts can play by even stricter rules, such as "only one touch per person" or "use both feet before getting rid of the ball."

Juggling

The skill used in Zelmo is called juggling, and players can practice it on their own. Juggling helps you develop a feel for the ball, while improving your concentration and "body rhythm." It also helps young players feel comfortable with the ball at many different angles and heights.

Try to keep the ball in the air as long as possible. Your foot should be bent slightly, with the toes pointing up; each touch should bring the ball up toward you. This foot position keeps the ball from going too high or falling away from you. Keep your eye on the ball; make sure your weight is low; maintain your balance (having your hands at your sides helps); and keep both your feet and thighs level, so the ball does not bounce away.

As with Zelmo, beginners can start by dropping the ball from the hands onto the foot or thigh, and letting the ball bounce in between. (If you're having a really tough time, catch the ball after each touch until you get the hang of it.) With confidence, you can flick the ball up to yourself; you can use your feet (inside, outside, and instep), thighs, and even your head. Set goals for yourself: 5 juggles without a miss, then 10, on up to . . . ?! Once you get good, try juggling as you move across the field. But don't forget to keep counting!

And if there is no soccer ball handy, don't worry. You can juggle practically anything, like a tennis ball or volleyball. Pele and other world-class players got their starts juggling oranges and old socks. (Some of them did it in the streets, which we don't recommend!)

We don't want to put any pressure on you, but the world record for juggles is over 15,000. And that's without bounces.

Soccer Tennis

Tennis, anyone?

This game is played exactly (well, sort of) like tennis, with two players on either side of a "net" (a bench turned sideways works best). Use cones to mark the sidelines and end lines of the "court." The object is to score against the other team by making them lose control of the ball out of bounds, or having it drop and roll between them so they can't hit it over the net. The two teammates can juggle the ball as many times as they want before hitting it over to the other side; the idea, of course, is to set up a shot that cannot be returned.

Beginners can serve by dropping the ball onto their own foot; more experienced players start by flicking the ball up to themselves.

Soccer Volleyball

This is a little harder than soccer tennis. For one thing, you've got four or more players on a team; for another, a volleyball net is high (you can use something lower, like a badminton net). But, just like soccer tennis and "real" volleyball, you're trying to keep the ball in the air on your side, and to deliver an unreturnable shot. As with soccer tennis, beginners serve by dropping the ball to themselves; experienced players start with the ball on the ground, and flick it to their own feet.

9

Pressure Training

Because much of soccer is played under pressure, here's a good way to work on ball control and pressure at the same time. Form a circle, with five or six players on the outside. Each player has a ball. One stands in the center of the circle, without a ball. In a predetermined direction (clockwise or counterclockwise), players on the outside serve balls to the one in the middle. They can be tosses or kicks to any part of the body. They can be easy or hard; they can be to the feet, chest, or head. The player in the center must control the ball, then pass it back to the server. When starting, give the player in the center plenty of time between serves; then increase the frequency with which balls are fed. This gets pretty tiring, so each person should spend only a minute or two in the middle before rotating out. For an even greater challenge, place a defender right behind the player in the middle. The defender starts out simply shadowing the player; later, the defender tries to win the ball.

3 Dribbling

Once you've mastered ball control, the next technique to work on is dribbling. It sounds gross, like something you do with your mouth, but it's just another name for the way you move the ball up and down the field. Dribbling simply means running with the ball.

When you start out, you'll probably kick the ball farther than you should. Soon, however, you'll be able to keep the ball close to you ("within playing distance"). You'll also be able to use both feet; to vary your speeds; and—best of all—to add a few fakes, throwing your opponents off guard before you blow past them.

In order to keep the ball close, you'll want to stay low to the ground. By shifting your weight to your legs, you can stop, start, and cut quicker than if you're standing straight up—and stopping, starting, and cutting are a few of the keys to good dribbling.

The most common form of dribbling involves the inside of the foot. It's natural—there's plenty of surface area, and by turning your foot slightly outward, it's easy to control where you want the ball to go. A good way to start feeling comfortable with your dribble is to stand with your legs spread shoulder-width apart, then knock the ball back and forth using the insides of your feet. Soon you'll develop a rhythm, and the ball will feel like it belongs between your feet.

Then, add forward movement. Dribbling should become part of your natural running motion: Kick the ball a few feet ahead, run after it, touch it while you're still running, then repeat the process.

If you keep doing this with your strong foot, of course, all you'll do is dribble in a straight line. That's fine if there's no one in your way. But in soccer, there's usually someone ahead of you. That's why it's important to learn to use both feet: It's a handy way of changing direction. You may feel awkward at first, but if you learn to use your weak foot as well as your strong one, you'll be a *much* better dribbler—and a much more valuable player overall.

Sometimes, of course, you *will* find no one in your path. That's the time to use a *speed dribble*. The best way to move quickly with the ball is to touch it with the outside of your foot. To do this correctly you must curve your foot inward just before it touches the ball, almost as if you were pigeon-toed. Because the field in front of you is open, you can push the ball farther ahead than when you use the inside of your foot. Still, be careful to keep the ball fairly close—and be sure to run (not walk!) after it.

For variety, you can also use the instep (laces) to dribble. This is not as accurate, because there is less surface area to meet the ball, and you're likely to kick it too hard, but it *is* another method of dribbling.

As you dribble, be sure to keep your upper body tilted slightly forward; this helps you protect the ball as much as possible. Your arms should be held slightly out at your sides, for balance.

Dribbling does *not* mean always going forward. Sometimes you'll have to move sideways (laterally), or even backward, because the field ahead is too crowded, or there's no one to receive your pass. Sometimes, even though there is someone in your way, you'll *want* to go forward. That's where fakes (also called "feints") come into play.

There are as many feints in soccer as there are soccer players. Every player develops his or her own style—moves that feel good, and natural. Some like to step over the ball, dip the shoulder on that side, then play it with the other foot. Some pull or drag the ball backward with the bottom of the foot, then quickly push it in a new direction. Some flick the ball over an opponent's foot in mid-dribble; some pretend to play the ball with one foot, then quickly use the other. You can also do an L move by dragging the ball with the bottom of your foot, then playing it with the inside of your foot (forming the letter *L,* either the right way or backward depending on which foot you use).

Here are a few other suggestions. Dribble to within a few feet of your opponent. Fake a kick—but instead step around the ball, plant your foot on the other side, then push the ball in the opposite direction with the outside of your step-around foot, and dribble quickly away. It's important to do this move quickly. Stay low over the ball for balance, and for maximum effect turn your hips and point your step-around foot in the direction opposite the one you plan to go. Finally, don't lift your foot too high over the ball; it slows you down, and affects your balance.

Another good feint is the hesitation move. As you dribble forward, with an opponent next to you, bring your foot over the ball and pause—without touching it. In one motion, bring that same foot back, behind the ball, then tap it forward. When your opponent hesitates as well, put on a burst of speed and start dribbling quickly down the field. The more you practice this, the easier it will be to maneuver at a quick pace.

Feel free to invent your own moves. The best ones involve some sort of deception with a body part that is not your feet. For example, a hip fake or dip of the shoulder suggests you're going one way when you really turn another, while a glance upfield with your eyes can momentarily distract your opponent.

Speaking of your eyes: Good dribblers do not need to look down at the ground. They *know* where the ball is: It's always within playing distance. They also know the grass is not going to move, but the players on the field will. By looking up as much as possible, dribblers are able to stay in command of the constant changes that take place during a soccer game. They might be ready to pass off, but suddenly a teammate is covered, so they dribble instead. Or in mid-dribble they see a teammate breaking free, and instantly send a through ball that leads to a goal. You can't do that if you're looking down. So try to get in the habit of dribbling with your head up.

One way to do that is . . .

The Finger Game

While you dribble in a confined area, ask a partner to hold up anywhere from one to five fingers, at random times. As soon as you see the fingers raised, shout out the number. It's hard at first. You'll probably move slowly, and only in a straight line. But as you grow confident that the ball won't skitter away, you'll pick up speed and move away from your partner. You'll keep your head up, because you know there's someplace other than the ground to look. Soon you'll be dribbling like a real soccer player!

Red Light, Green Light

This is a good game for learning to dribble at different speeds. One person stands in the middle of a circle. When he says "Green light!" players dribble forward, or to the side; when he says "Red light!" they stop the ball dead. Anyone caught moving after one second must sit down. The idea is to start and stop quickly, with the ball always under control.

Simon Says

Again one player directs the action, while everyone else obeys his or her commands. Simon can say: "Dribble forward!" "Change direction!" "Go backward!" "Dribble sideways!" "Dribble with the outside of your foot!" "Use the inside of your foot!" "Stop the ball dead, then dribble as fast as you can into space!" And, of course, if he or she does not say "Simon says," no one should move! (This game develops good listening skills, too.)

Follow the Leader

One player leads everyone on a run. As the leader speeds up, slows down, or changes direction, everyone must follow exactly in his or her path. The catch, of course, is that everyone has a soccer ball, so it's not as easy as it sounds. (It's important to look up when following the leader, so this shows dribblers how to "see the whole field.")

Relay Races

Everyone loves relay races. To practice dribbling, you and a few friends can form pairs. Someone yells "Go!" and the first person in each pair takes off. As soon as that person returns, the second person goes. (This means the first person must stop the ball dead on the line—using the ball control skills you learned in the previous section.) The team that finishes first—again, stopping the ball dead—is the winner.

When that becomes easy, you can add other challenges. Instead of dribbling in a straight line, make a few turns. The next time you go, insist that each touch of the ball must be with the alternate foot. The *next* time, do the entire relay race using your weak foot.

Crash!

To practice dribbling at different speeds, four players can start in the middle of the four sides of a big square. When someone says "Go!" all four dribble quickly to the middle.

You'll probably all arrive at the same time. Because crashing into each other is not smart (although it might look funny), you'll have to slow down, and maybe change direction. Then, as soon as you get clear, speed up again and dribble to the opposite side.

The Circle Game

This practice game uses the center circle. Get a few friends; everyone must have a soccer ball. Start dribbling anywhere, but stay inside the circle. You'll have to change direction often to avoid each other. That's good—but so is speeding up and dribbling "into space" whenever you've got room.

Fake It

A good way to prac-
tice your fakes is
with a partner.
Measure out a dis-
tance—20 or 30
yards is best. Your
job is to dribble at
your partner, then
put on such a good
fake that you blaze
on past and get to the
other side without losing the
ball. Remember to use different parts of your body—your
eyes, head, and hips in particular—and not just your feet.

Over the Goal Line

Mark out a field about 40 yards long and 20 yards wide. Use existing lines, or create goal lines at each end with cones. 4-v.-4 is the best number to play this game, although other numbers work, too. The object is to score by dribbling the ball over the goal line. You must have full control of the ball as you cross the goal line, or else the goal does not count. It is the defenders' job to make this difficult, so after the ball has been passed around a bit, the player with the ball must pick the correct time and space to dribble. This game is good not only for dribbling and taking on opponents, but also for supporting, passing, changing the direction of play, vision, and defense.

Crows and Cranes

Form two teams: Crows and Cranes. One team spreads out, all facing the same direction, 30–40 yards from a goal line or end line; every player has a ball. The other team stands 10 yards behind them; no one has a ball. At a signal, all the players with soccer balls must dribble toward that line; the other team, without soccer balls, tries to catch and tag them. Keep score of the number of players caught. This is excellent for speed dribbling (and, of course, speed, period!).

All Around the Circle

Form a circle. Player A begins dribbling around the outside. When Player A touches someone in the circle (Player B), she continues dribbling—and Player B dribbles in the opposite direction. The first person to get back to the empty spot stays there; the other player becomes "it."

Tag

Tag is an old standby, but with soccer there are a couple of fun variations. One is "chain tag," where players dribble in a small area. The one player without the ball, who is "it," tries to tag teammates. A tagged teammate gets rid of the ball, locks hands with "it," and forms a chain. The chain tries to tag players, and grow. As the chain grows, the area used can also shrink. This is a great way to practice dribbling, because the players with the ball must use many different moves and changes of direction to avoid the chain.

I Got There First!

You need only one other person for this game. Set up two cones, about 12 yards apart. You start with a ball in the middle, about 10 yards back from the cones. Your friend starts without a ball, in the same position on the other side of the cones. Your job is to dribble forward and sideways, using as many moves as you can, then touch either cone with the ball—and do it before your friend, without the ball, touches that same cone with his or her hand. It's up to you to try a couple of fakes (feints), then burst in the other direction toward the opposite cone, all the while controlling the ball. Hopefully you will catch your friend leaning the wrong way, unable to react in time. Then give your friend the ball. Keep track of how many times you "score" with the ball, and without it; have your friend do the same.

4 Passing

Now that you feel comfortable with the ball—and know how to dribble it, *and* keep it away from opponents—it's time to give it up.

That's right: The best soccer players are the ones who take the *fewest* touches on the ball.

Individual skills are very important, but the last time we looked, soccer was a game of 11 players on a team. (We know, there are only four or five on a small-sided team, but that's still a lot more than 1-v.-1.) It takes an entire team to score a goal, and that's why knowing how to pass is crucial.

The quickest way to move a soccer ball up and down the field is by passing it. The ball moves a lot faster going from one player to another in the air, even on the ground, than it does when only one person is controlling it. Good passes send teammates off on breakaways, or help them get 2-on-1s. Good passes catch defenders out of position, forcing them to run desperately to catch up. Good passes lead to shots on goals. Good passes are an essential part of good soccer.

There are as many ways to pass as there are to dribble. As with dribbling, each player develops an individual passing style. But the passer should always look up before striking the ball, for two reasons: (1) To make sure the receiver is actually making the run the passer thinks is being made, and (2) to make certain the receiver is not being marked so closely that the pass might be intercepted.

The Main Types of Passes

Short Passes

If a teammate is 5 to 20 yards away, you'll want to make a short pass. (Anything closer than 5 yards and you might as well keep the ball yourself.) A short pass is one that stays on the ground, making it easy to handle. A short pass is struck neither too hard (in which case it will bounce off the shins) or too soft (in which case it might get intercepted).

When making a short pass, first "lock" the ankles by tightening the muscles of your lower foot. (You can practice doing that without the ball. Have a parent or friend try to twist your foot. If the foot flops all around like a fish, your ankle is not locked. If your foot is firm, your ankle is securely locked.)

At the same time your ankle is locked, turn the kicking foot sideways. The nonkicking foot should be 6–8 inches from the ball, pointing in the direction you want your pass to go.

Then bring your foot back slightly. Leaning over the ball, and keeping the sole of your foot parallel to the ground, you should then make contact near the middle of the ball. The inside of the front part of your foot should hit the ball. If it hits your ankle, your foot is not forward enough.

Short passes should be struck with the inside of the foot. If you use your instep (laces), you'll hit it too hard. If you use your toes, you'll lack preci-sion (*never hit the ball with your toes in soccer, for any reason!*). If you hit it too high, you'll just scuff it off to the side; too low, and it's likely to rise in the air. Leaning over the ball helps keep it on the ground. After strik-ing the ball, make sure you follow through (keep the foot moving for-ward), with the ankle still locked. This gives the ball a bit more power.

You can practice with a stationary ball (one that's stand-ing still). During a game, however, you'll most likely be hit-ting moving soccer balls. To make sure you hit a moving ball well, make sure that your "plant foot" (the one that's *not* kicking) is next to the ball. Beginners sometimes pass when they're too far away from the ball. That means they sacrifice both power and accuracy.

If you get very good at short passing, you might want to try using the outside of the foot. *Be sure your ankle is locked.* This pass is less accurate, and should be used only when a defender prevents you from using the inside of your foot. But it's certainly a good way to get the ball to a teammate when you're under pressure.

Chips

Chips are medium-length passes, to teammates who are 20 to 30 yards away. A "chip" means the ball is lifted in the air, over other players' heads. Try not to make medium-length passes waist- or chest-high; they're easy to intercept.

To chip a ball, you should use your instep (laces). You still lock the ankle, but this time you approach the ball straight, or at a slight angle, and strike it a little lower than you would for a short pass. Again you follow through, but this time your foot should curl upward, not sideways. (If you want to put backspin on the ball, do not follow through.) You should also lean back when you make this medium-length pass, and keep your arms at your side for balance.

Long Passes

If you've ever seen a professional game, you know older players can pass the ball clear across the field. It will be a while before you're able to do so—but it's never too early to learn how to make a long pass.

As with a chip, you'll lock your ankle and use your laces. As with the other types of passing, you'll make sure your plant (nonkicking) foot is next to the ball. But this time you'll *really* lean back, get under the ball, and follow through, with a strong upward motion. Like chips, long passes should be higher than other players' heads, so they won't get picked off.

Wall Passes

These are very effective passes, of short and medium length, on the ground. At the same time you dribble toward a defender, a teammate is moving toward you out of the defender's range. When you're close to the defender—but not too close for an interception—pass the ball to your teammate's feet, then run past the defender to receive a quick pass back. Your teammate's pass should come right back to you, first time ("one touch"). That's where the term *wall pass* originates, because it's like receiving a rebound off a wall. You can practice wall passes with a friend, first without and then with an opponent, until they become almost automatic.

Passing in Pairs

Passing with a partner is the best way to practice, but it gets awfully boring pretty quickly. One way to spice up the action is to add competitive elements. See how many passes you and your friend can make before someone messes up. Or count the number of passes you complete in a predetermined amount of time, for instance 30 seconds. If you've got an even number of friends, turn it into a competition: You and one person against other twosomes. To be fair, don't forget to rotate partners!

Go Fish

If you want to practice different types of passes, one right after the other, grab a few soccer balls, a soccer buddy, and a fishing net (yes, you read correctly). Line up the balls near each other; have your friend stand 10–20 yards away. Your friend moves the net to different heights, and at different angles; your job is to pass the ball into the net each time. This helps develop the habit of making different passes (high, low, hard, soft) each time—which is exactly what happens during a game.

Two-Line Passing

One of the easiest ways to practice passing is to get two or three players in two lines, facing each other, 10–20 yards apart. The first player passes to the facing player; as soon as he makes his pass, he runs to the end of the opposite line. (This is because it's never a good idea to just watch what you've just done; you want to "follow your pass.") The next player controls the ball, then passes it to the new first person in line. Keep going; count how many passes you can make without fouling up.

When you've reached your goal—20 in a row without a mistake, for example—you can add new elements. You can try to control the ball with one foot, then pass it with the opposite foot. You can try to make every pass "one touch" (without a controlling touch). You can even try to make every pass with your weak foot (that will look pretty funny in the beginning!).

For a greater challenge, add another two lines—this time crisscrossing the two that you've already got. (In other words, you'll have two lines facing each other going north and south, two others facing each other east and west.) Using two balls, players pass the ball to the person facing them, then race to the end of the opposite line—but they're doing it while two other players are doing the exact same thing. You've got to keep your head up to avoid collisions, but you've also got to watch the ball, to make sure your passes and controls are crisp and clean.

Circle Around

Another good way to practice lots of passes in a row is to form a circle, with one player in the middle. Each player on the outside has a ball. One by one, in turn, they pass to the person in the middle, who passes right back. The better you get at passing, the quicker the passes can come.

For a variation, have only two balls on the outside of the circle. As soon as the player in the middle makes a pass (to someone *without* the ball), the other player with the ball passes to the middle. The one in the middle then passes *that* ball to someone new. It can get pretty complicated—but remember, soccer is a game for smart people!

Once you've got *that* down, put a defender on the back of the person in the middle, who now has got to make passes under a bit more pressure.

Boom!

This is similar to the circle exercise above, except now you've got *two* circles, each with equal numbers of players. One person stands in the middle of each circle. The idea is for the player in the middle to receive a pass from, and pass the ball back to, each person on the outside. The team that completes its circle first sits down and yells "Boom!" Repeat, until everyone has had a chance to be the receiver in the middle. (NOTE: You can play this two ways: Using one ball per circle, in which case the player in the middle passes to the next player each time, or using one ball for each player, in which case the person in the middle passes back to the *same* person on the outside.)

Knockout

This is a fun, strategic game. Mark out a fairly large area. Any number can play, as long as each has a soccer ball. Players begin by knocking their ball as close to the center as possible; from then on, the idea is to knock every other player's ball out of the area, by striking it with your own. This game emphasizes both accuracy and power. If you hit your ball too hard and miss another player's, you might bang your own ball out of the area. If you strike it too soft, however, you set yourself up for someone else to knock you out. The winner is the last player left.

5-v.-2

This is such an excellent training exercise for passing (and defending) that many teams use it as a warm-up before games. Get five players in a circle (four in a square also works); two others go in the middle. The five pass the ball around, using no more than two touches each. Most of the passes should be to the outside; occasionally, if there is a clear lane available, it can go through the middle (those passes are riskier). The two players in the middle try to intercept the ball. Because the two in the middle work as a team, the one who is there the longest (not the one who "wins" the ball) goes to the outside after an interception, and the player who made the pass that was intercepted moves to the middle. The more you play this game, the better you get. It won't take long before you're able to keep the ball going around the outside for several minutes at a time. The players in the middle get frustrated—but pretty soon they figure out how to work together to win the ball, too.

Soccer Tag

This is just like regular tag—except the player who is "it" dribbles the ball, and "tags" other players by passing the ball at their legs. This game is great for passing accuracy. Be sure to set a time limit. Everyone gets a chance to be "it" once; the winner is the person who tags the most people while "it."

Another variation is "freeze tag." Every player except one who is "it" has a ball, and dribbles in a grid. When "it" tags someone, that player must stop and hold the ball over his or her head, with feet spread apart. The only way to get "unfrozen" is if a teammate passes the ball through that player's legs.

Passing in Space

Soccer is a game of space—no, not outer space; *field* space. To practice short, medium, and long passing, pair up. You and your partner pass the ball to one another—but you should vary your short, medium, and long passes. This means you both must watch each other closely all the time, because it does not make much soccer sense to pass to a teammate who is not ready to receive the ball. You can run away, then "check back" (return) for a pass. You can chip the ball over an imaginary opponent's head. You can do anything you want, in fact, as long as your pass is smart and sharp. (This practice game is especially fun when you've got several "pairs" passing at the same time. Now you've got to watch out for traffic, and *still* make sure you're giving the right pass.)

Interception!

Several players divide into pairs. Within a small area, they pass to each other. One player is the "interceptor." He tries

to intercept the ball before it gets to the receiver. Obviously, the pairs of passers have to move around; they have to make their passes at the right moment (to avoid being intercepted), and they have to strike the passes with enough power so that they are not easy to intercept. This is a game with plenty of movement, and lots of challenges for everyone.

A variation is to divide into two groups of five to six players each, 15–20 yards apart. One person stands in the middle ("no-man's-land"). Players on each side can pass the ball laterally (sideways) among themselves; when the time is right, they attempt to make a long pass in the air to the other side. A player in no-man's-land who successfully intercepts the ball gets to replace the one who made the pass.

Short-Short-Long

Most passes in soccer are short; long passes are much rarer. To get in the habit of making more short passes than long, three players can knock the ball around. Two of them are close together; they pass short between themselves. Every so often, however, they can look up and hit a long pass to the third teammate. When that happens, the player who hit the long pass follows it. Then he and the "long" receiver play short together, while the other player now becomes the one waiting for a long pass.

Five Passes

You and your friends can divide into two equal teams. Set boundaries—half-field or less works well. There are no goals to shoot at; instead, the "goal" of each team is to make five passes in a row without the other team touching the ball (even a toenail counts as a touch). When you've got five completed passes in a row, your team gets a point. Play to a predetermined number, such as three or five.

Short-Sided Soccer

Short-sided games (3-v.-3, 4-v.-4, or 5-v.-5) are one of the best ways to learn how to pass. Use a smaller field; put cones five steps apart as goals at each end. Divide the teams equally, then play. Short-sided soccer is a great way to practice all your skills, but it's your passing that will probably improve most. With small numbers, you can't hold on to the ball—you'll get too tired. But in order for your passes to work, you've got to move to receive it back just as soon as you've gotten rid of it. You'll do a decent amount of running "off" (without) the ball; you shouldn't do too much running with it. The idea is to let the ball do most of the work, and the way to do that is by passing.

Short-sided games can be adapted to work on particular passing skills. For example, if you want to get good at quick passes, you can limit the entire game to "three touch," or even "two touch." (No players get more than three or two touches before they must pass—and that includes the first touch to control the ball.) If you want to work on your weak foot, you can say that participants must pass only with their weak foot. (This will look kind of goofy at first, but eventually it will resemble real soccer.)

You can add tactical ideas, too. For instance, a team must complete an "overlap" (one player moving forward from behind, to receive a lead pass) or a "give-and-go" (a pass that is immediately returned by the receiver to the first player) before shooting.

As with so many of these drills and games, you can adapt short-sided soccer any way you wish. The only thing stopping you from creating new games is the limit of your own imagination.

Random Goal Game

Set up a series of "cone goals" (five steps apart) randomly, in half the field. Each goal should be set at a different angle. Split up into two teams. Either team can shoot at any of the goals. But the only way a goal counts is if the ball is passed through the cones, on the ground—*and* if a teammate receives and controls it on the other side.

Small Goals, Big Goal

Another excellent game involves setting up two small cone goals, 25–30 yards from the goal line. You'll need at least five players on each team to play. In order to score the only goal that "counts"—the one on the large, regulation-size goal with a goalkeeper—a team must first pass the ball through either of the small goals. As soon as this is done, that team turns and attacks the large goal, and the other team defends it (while also attempting to pass through one of the two small ones). This is great for passing. You're not only trying to pass the ball through the small goals, but you are working the ball across the field because you've got two small goals at opposite ends. Then, after succeeding there, you pass it around to get a shot on the big one. (Of course, at the same time you're also working on shooting, defending, and making the transition from offense to defense.)

Long Ball

This game teaches distance, accuracy, and power in passing, as well as receiving and controlling the ball. Players spread out in pairs. One player has a ball; the other player makes a run to receive a long pass. The passer gets 5 points for reaching the player all the way in the air; 3 points for getting it there with one bounce; and 1 point for two bounces. Keep track of your points.

Pass and Think

Several players form a circle (the center circle works well for this). Player A passes to Player B on the opposite side of the circle, then follows the pass immediately by running to where B is. Player B, meanwhile, has already passed to Player C, and is following his or her own pass. The ball moves quickly, so everyone must control the ball before passing, must make crisp passes, and must be alert at all times.

Give Me the Ball!

It is very important to make passes at the right moment. This means not only when you want to pass, but when the receiver is in the proper position to receive the ball. No defender should be able to win your pass. To practice this, kick around with your partner. There should be plenty of eye contact, and also verbal communication. Right before you move to get the ball, yell "Yes!" or "Hit me!" or "I'm open!" Specific directions are even better: "Hit me left!" "Up wing!" "Center!"

Hot Potato

Here is a great way to develop quick passing skills. Get several players in a circle. Pass the ball back and forth as quickly as possible. Set a time limit. Whoever has the ball when time is called has to sit out. If the ball is in motion, the player who is about to receive sits. The last player left is the winner.

By the Numbers

Here is a passing game that also makes you look, listen, and think. Get several friends—four to six will do—and give each a number. Then start moving around half-field, and passing. The thing is, each pass must be made to the next player in numerical order (1, 2, 3, etc., then back to 1). This means you must constantly be aware of both the player who will pass to you, and the one to whom you will pass. If you are the receiver, you must get yourself in a supporting position before the passer passes. If you are the passer, you must position the ball so you can pass it easily and quickly. This becomes particularly difficult when you add a restriction, such as "two-touch passing" (no more than two touches by anyone, including the first touch used to control the ball).

So how does this hone "listening" skills? In soccer, a player in position to receive the ball often calls for it. The more communication you can make in this exercise, the better it will work.

Seeing Double

Two players, two soccer balls—what could be simpler?

But this exercise is far more difficult than it sounds. You and a friend each have a soccer ball—and pass it back and forth to each other, simultaneously. Start from a standing position; once you can do that without too much chaos, try the same thing while moving. You've got to do a lot almost simultaneously—striking the ball, receiving it, watching where your target is, and keeping both your balance and wits. Then again, soccer is a game in which many things happen at once.

Under Pressure

It's easy to control the ball when there's no one around. But what about when you are under pressure?

Pressure can come in the form of a command from a teammate. You must listen to what's being said, then react quickly. For example, the command "Hold!" means you should control the ball, then hold onto it yourself. "Turn!" means you should control it, but turn upfield. "Back!" means you should control it once, then pass it right back—or, under extreme pressure, strike it first time.

To learn how to control the ball under pressure, have a partner serve you passes, and tell you what to do (hopefully, with enough advance notice that you can actually do it). Then, add a defender on your back. The defender should play passive (easy) defense at first, then later actually try to intercept the ball.

Finally, the receiver can get in the middle of a circle, with a defender close behind. Some of the players on the outside of the circle have a ball; others do not. In a clockwise or counterclockwise rotation, they strike passes to the receiver, and give a command. The receiver must either play the ball back, or to another free player. It's not easy—but listening and looking are as much a part of passing as actually striking the ball.

Soccer Croquet

Use cones to create a series of "gates" throughout the soccer field. The idea is to pass through all the gates in order, and finish with a successful shot on goal. Some shots (passes through the gates) will be long; others will be short. Of course, as in real croquet, if an opponent's ball lies in your way, feel free to shoot at it and knock it to the side.

Soccer Golf

This does not actually involve passing to a partner, but the idea is the same. Besides, it's so much fun we thought we'd mention it here.

You and your friends can set up a "golf course" anywhere there is lots of space and varied terrain (open fields, woods, hills, maybe a river). Designate certain "tees" and "holes" (cones). Vary your course. Some holes should be close, others far away; some should be straightaways, others doglegs. The idea is to reach the cone in as few passes as possible. This is a great game for practicing all kinds of passes: long balls for distance, chips over obstacles, short passes for accurate "putts."

If you're feeling particularly evil, you can add another element: Try to knock your opponent's ball out of the way. Let's say you're both close to the cone, and it's your turn. Instead of shooting yourself, you can take the chance of aiming for his ball, and blasting it away.

Soccer golf has three advantages over the real version: It doesn't take nearly as long to play. You don't have to carry clubs. And there's never a chance of losing your ball!

5 Shooting

Controlling the ball, dribbling, and passing are great—but what's the whole idea of the game? Scoring more goals than the other team! And the only way to do that is to shoot!

Shooting is perhaps the most enjoyable part of soccer. There is nothing more satisfying than striking a ball so hard it nearly rips the back of the net—or so sweetly it sneaks past the keeper as if it had eyes of its own. (Special note to goalkeepers: We know there is nothing more satisfying to *you* than stopping those shots. Don't worry—you'll get your own chapter soon!)

Shooting is not a whole lot different from passing. You use the inside of your foot, the laces, and sometimes the outside of the foot. (You can also, on rare occasions, use your head.) The difference is, you're aiming not for a teammate's foot, or a vast amount of space, but for a small corner of the goal. And that tiny piece of property is protected by the one player allowed to use his hands.

That's why in shooting, accuracy is so much more important than power. It's common to think that the harder you shoot, the more likely you are to score. Not true! If you develop a solid, accurate shot, you'll be celebrating a lot more than the player who blasts every ball as hard as possible (usually those blasts will fly wide, or sail over the top).

The best place to aim is low, and to the far corner. You want to shoot low because most keepers hate to dive. (It's tempting, of course, to try to chip the ball over the heads of small keepers. But those goalies will grow, so it's smarter to get in the habit of shooting low as soon as you can.) Another reason for shooting low is that if you miskick the ball and it goes high, it's still got a chance. However, if you aim for the upper twine and kick high, you might send the ball into orbit.

The best way to make sure your shot stays low is to stretch the ankle, so that you strike the ball with a flat surface. The more your toe points forward underneath the ball, the greater the chance you will lift it off the ground.

And why should you shoot to the far corner? That's where the greatest amount of open space is. Most keepers protect their near post; the far side is yours. The best way to shoot to the far corner is to make sure your foot swings across your body (instead of poking the ball forward with the toes, which is a big no-no!).

Your body should be well-balanced when you shoot. That means making sure your

"plant" (nonkicking) foot is even with the ball, about six inches away. If you're too far away when you shoot, you're likely to either scuff it or sky it. The toes of your plant foot should be aimed in the direction of your kick.

At the same time, the toes of your kicking foot should be pointed down, and your ankle locked.

You also need to lean over the ball. Keeping your body low during the shot helps keep the ball low, too. The straighter your body is, the more chance there is of your shot going over the top. In addition to keeping your ankle locked (we know, we said it already, but it bears repeating!), make sure to hold your head steady.

As noted before, you don't have to kill the ball. A good shot will provide its own power. Think of most shots as short punches. In most cases, accuracy is as important as power.

Your eyes should be down, concentrating on the ball and the area around it. You don't need to look at the goal—it's not going to move. But the ball will be bouncing, and there will be defenders in your way, so you should look there instead of up.

A common problem is that shooters want to watch the ball go in the net. Don't worry—you don't need to see it. The roar of your teammates will tell you you've scored. The more you keep your head down—even during the follow-through—the greater the chance you will hear that roar!

As with passing, follow-through is important. This is where the power in your shot comes from; it does *not* come from pulling your foot way back and blasting the you-know-what out of the ball. Good follow-through means swinging all the way through the ball. The best shooters even add a little hop after their shot.

Once you've shot, follow the ball all the way to the goal. It's amazing how many goals you can score after the keeper bobbles your first shot, or it caroms off the goalpost.

After you've gotten down the basics, you can add variety to your shots. If you're right-footed and want to bend the ball to the right, strike through it a bit to the inside of center, with the inside or outside of the foot. If you want to bend the ball to the left, strike through it a bit to the outside of center, again with the inside or outside of the instep.

Another good shot is the volley (kicking the ball while it is still in the air). Good preparation and timing is essential when you volley the ball. You should face the approaching ball, and point your nonkicking foot toward it. With your kicking foot, point the toes down and keep the ankle locked. Lift the kicking foot, and strike through the center of the ball. For a side volley (a ball bouncing to your side), turn the body and punch through the ball, again keeping your toes down and ankle rigid.

All these shots can be practiced using a commercial device consisting of a ball and rope. You hold the rope in your hand, and practice kicking the ball however you wish: inside of the foot, instep, outside, even volleys. The ball flies away and then gets yanked back to you by the rope. This is a great way to get used to how a shot ought to feel, even if no one else is around to help serve and fetch.

Of course, you don't need a full-size goal to practice shooting. Sporting goods stores sell small, portable goals that can be set up in any backyard. You can even tie a sheet between two trees, hang a tire from a branch, lie a garbage can on its side . . . you get the idea. Living far away from a soccer field does not mean you can't work on shooting. On the contrary, it's a skill you can drill anywhere.

Two final ideas to remember: (1) During a match you don't need to see the goal in order to shoot. All you need is for the *ball* to have room to score. Get in the habit of pushing the ball to one side, then releasing a quick shot. Goals are often scored not because they're great shots, but because they catch the keeper by surprise. (2) Whenever you practice shooting, make sure the ball is moving. After all, that's what the ball will be doing during a game!

1-v.-1

If you can score on a small goal, then shooting on a big one will be a piece of cake. A good way to practice shooting is to go 1-v.-1 with a friend, on a field 20 yards long. "Goals" can be cones, five steps apart. Or you can use friends' legs as goals—just make sure they are spread wide enough for you to score through. (This is a very tiring game, so play for just a minute or so. Then change places with the friends who served as "goals.")

For variety, set up one small goal using cones, five steps apart. You and your friend still go 1-v.-1— but this time either you or your opponent can shoot from either side. You'll get a good workout, and plenty of practice getting past your friend, then firing a quick shot on the run.

3-v.-1

Here is a good game for four people. Divide into 3-v.-1; set up one cone as your goal, which the one player defends. (That player should not be so close that he or she can touch it, however.) The other three players pass the ball around, waiting for a good shot. As soon as you've got the shot, take it. If it knocks over the cone, you get a point. If the defender wins the ball, through an interception or tackle, he or she joins the three, and the player who made the pass becomes the defender.

More Small Goals

Here's another good game that doesn't require large goals. You can get plenty of shooting practice by spreading four or five sets of cones across half the field (again, these "goals" should be five steps apart). You and your friends divide into two equal teams. Either team can score on any of the goals, from any angle. This encourages lots of shots, as well as plenty of movement and passing.

A Few Shooting Exercises

When you practice shooting using a full-size goal, it's no fun to race in alone on the poor goalie (especially for the keeper!). You'll become a much better shooter if you add a defender into the mix.

In one exercise, two players start at the top of the penalty box, where the penalty arc meets the line. One person stands behind them, serving a ball into the middle (either in the air or on the ground). The player who wins the ball immediately becomes the shooter; the other person defends. The player with the ball goes to goal, and tries to shoot; the other one tries to stop the shooter.

Another exercise begins with two players standing next to each other, 30 yards from the goal. A third person serves the ball from the goal line, in the air or on the ground. Again, the player who wins the ball tries to shoot; the other one defends.

A variation has one player standing next to the goal, serving the ball to another player 30 yards out. As soon as the server strikes the ball, the server races out to become the defender. The player who receives the ball must control it, then try to fire a shot as quickly as possible.

The most basic shooting drill involves a shooter standing in line with a ball, facing one person whose back is to the goal. The shooter passes to that person, who immediately feeds the ball laterally (sideways) or forward to the shooter, who then fires first time (or after one touch to control.)

However, there are endless other ways to shoot. Some do not involve a pass, but are challenging nonetheless. For example, the ball can be served with a toss, over the head of the shooter, who must (a) move onto it as soon as he or she sees it, then (b) control a bouncing ball, and (c) fire on goal.

You can also place one defender just inside the 18-yard line (top of the penalty box), with the shooter just beyond the line. The shooter can start with the ball, or else receive it from someone on the side or behind. The defender cannot cross the line, but can move side to side trying to prevent a shot. The shooter cannot cross the line either, and so must maneuver sideways trying to get a good shot off. Once the shooter has an opening, he or she should shoot. It is not helpful to wait for the "perfect" opportunity, because that may never come. As noted earlier, you don't need a huge opening to take a shot. You don't even need to see an open net. All the ball needs is an unobstructed path!

If you are alone you can get all the shooting practice you need, provided you have several soccer balls. Place the soccer balls—as many as you can round up—a couple of feet apart, at a challenging distance from the goal. Then start firing on net (with or without a keeper). Bang, bang, bang— one right after the other. This helps improve quickness of shooting, and also trains you to shoot when fatigued. It's also good for repetition: The more shots you take in a row, the easier it is to get in the "shooting groove."

Cones, Cones, and More Cones

Set 5–10 cones along a line; do the same along another line, 30–40 yards apart. Divide into two teams. Each team tries to knock down all the other team's cones; the first to finish wins. There will be lots of shots—but accuracy counts!

You can also use cones in a full-size goal. Stand six right

next to each other along the goal line in one corner; put another six in a row in the opposite corner. Divide players into two groups, and alternate shots. One team starts at the left edge of the penalty area; the other starts at the right. Players take one touch, then shoot. The object is for your team to knock over all six cones—the ones at the far post— before the other team knocks over theirs. This is a great way to practice shooting low, to the corner, and hard.

Dribble Before You Shoot

Set up an obstacle course, with several cones that you must dribble at, then around. You should be moving forward, but not always in a straight line. The cones should not all be the same distance apart. Fifteen yards beyond the last cone, set up two more cones, four steps apart, as a "goal." The idea is to dribble through the obstacle course, under control, then sprint a couple of steps past the final cone and score on the "goal." You can time yourself, to see how you improve (if you miss the goal, don't count your time), or you and a few friends can compete against each other for time.

Four-Goal Game

In a small area—say, half of half-field—set up four goals, using cones (each goal is five steps apart). Two of the goals go north-south; the other two go east-west. Form two equal teams. Each team shoots at two goals (one straight ahead, the other to the side); they defend the other two. Each goal that is scored counts as 1 point; play to a predetermined number, such as 11. Remember, in order to count the ball must go in on the ground. If it's in the air, it's no good.

Two Small Goals, One Large

This works best when you've got at least eight players. Divide into two equal teams. One team starts shooting at two small goals (cones), which are placed near the side-lines about 20–30 yards from the end line. The other team starts shooting at the large goal (with a goalie in it). The only time a point is scored is when the ball goes in the big goal—but (after the first time) the only way a team gets to shoot on the big goal is by scoring on the lit-tle goal. In other words, as soon as your team scores on the little goal, you turn around and start shooting on the big goal, and the other team defends it. There is plenty of passing in this game, along with lots of shots on both small and large goals.

Shooting Wars

Place two portable goals near each other, about 30 yards apart (be careful as you move them!). Play 3-v.-3 or 4-v.-4 (plus keepers). Because the goals are so close, you'll have plenty of opportunities to fire—virtually every person who touches the ball is within shooting range. But because it is so confined, very few of the shots will be clear. You will learn to shoot quickly, whenever you have a chance. If you've got enough players, you can make three teams. Each "game" is one goal: As soon as one team scores, the losers sit and the third team plays.

A variation of this game is to use no goalkeepers. That makes for a totally wide-open game—and enables you to experience the thrill of scoring over and over again.

Three Goals, Two Goalkeepers

Here is a creative use of goals (and goalkeepers). Make a circle; in the center, set up three cones in a triangular shape, so you have three "goals." Put two keepers in the middle; their job is to defend all three goals. There are six players in the circle. Start with one ball. They pass the ball around the circle and then shoot from outside. They can also dribble in, and try to score on the ground past one of the keepers. The reason there are two goalies is that as soon as one shot is taken, the person on the other side of the circle who gets the ball can also shoot.

Pitch-Back

One of the least appealing parts of shooting is fetching the ball. Forget about what happens when you miss the goal entirely; even if you score, you've got to jog over, reach down, and pull the ball out of the back of the net. That's why we're big fans of a commercial product that teaches shooting *without* fetching. It's smaller than a regular goal, but elastic netting covers the entire front. Every shot—every shot on goal, that is—gets rebounded right back at you. How's that for service!

6 Heading

Should you head a soccer ball?

Sure! It's a skill experienced players use from time to time, in defending, passing, and even shooting.

Should you spend lots of time practicing heading?

No! Studies have shown that heading—if done properly, and in limited amounts—is safe. You won't knock yourself out, or knock yourself silly, by occasionally heading a soccer ball.

So let's figure out what "proper heading" and "limited amounts" mean.

The proper way to head a soccer ball is to strike it at the hairline (the part of your head where the hair begins). You should *not* use the top of your head or (ha!) your nose to head.

Heading actually involves the entire upper body: The more power you have with your upper body, the better header you'll be. You should arch back (by pushing your chest forward), then "throw your eyes at the ball." That's just a phrase—but if you imagine yourself attacking the ball with your entire head, you'll get the idea.

If you learn to head that way, you won't get hurt—and your head won't hurt.

"Limited amounts" means practicing heading a few minutes, every so often. Most importantly, it means that you should not begin heading practice until heading becomes a normal part of the games you play. If you're still at an age when the ball is not kicked high enough to head, you do not need to practice this skill.

Types of Headers

There are several different types of headers. A pass to a teammate should be soft enough to be handled, and accurate enough not to be intercepted. A header that is a shot on goal should be hard—and you should aim it down. Ideally, a shot that's headed should bounce on the goal line (those are the types that give goalies fits). And a header that is a defensive clear should go "high and wide"—in other words, as far up and out to the nearest sideline as possible. Whatever you do, don't head into the middle of the field: That's an invitation to interception!

Practicing the Basics

A good way to practice heading is to start by holding the ball yourself, a few feet from your head. Arch your upper body back, then thrust your head at the ball as you hold it. You'll know you had correct form if you almost knock it out of your hands, and if it doesn't hurt your head at all.

When you know what a good header feels like, try it from a kneeling position. Have a partner hold the ball a few inches away from your head. Arch back, then—yep— "throw your eyes at the ball." This allows you to feel exactly where on your head the ball should hit.

Next, your partner can stand a few feet away, and gently toss the ball into the air. Again, arch back and head. Aim your headers directly into your partner's hands.

Finally, add a defender in front of you. The defender should stand still at first; all you have to do is jump high, and head the ball back. As you get the hang of jumping and heading, have the defender jump, too. Now you've got to make sure you outjump him or her. Finally, the defender can jump *and* attempt to head the ball as well.

Along with good jumping ability, timing becomes very important. Be sure to time your jump so you meet the ball at its height. If you learn to leap when *you* think you've got the best chance of heading the ball, you'll win more than your share of headers.

Back and Forth

Once you're standing, your partner can get a little farther away, and toss the ball to you. Soon, you will both start running: Your partner backward, you forward. Head every toss back to your partner's hands. After a few headers, switch places.

For a challenge, you and a friend can head back and forth. See how many times you can head it to each other before messing up.

You and a few friends can also get in a circle, and practice keeping the ball in the air with your heads. Remember, don't spend too long doing this. All it takes is a few minutes of practice.

Short-Short-Long

This heading game involves three players. Line up so that one player stands in the middle, closer to one and farther from the other. The middle player starts by tossing the ball to the nearer player, who heads it back to the tosser. That middle player heads it again to the near player, who then heads a l-o-n-g ball over the middle to the third player. The ball is then headed back to the middle. Get a rhythm going—see how many short-short-long headers you can do in a row without messing up.

Circle Heading

This exercise is as simple as it sounds. One player gets in the middle of a circle. Players on the outside take turns throwing the ball to the player in the middle, who heads it back to them. Players on the outside can also try heading it back to the middle. See how many times you can do this before the ball lands somewhere else!

The Heading Game

Here's a game that can be played just like soccer. Divide into two teams: 5-v.-5, 10-v.-10, it doesn't matter. If you've got low numbers, bring the goals closer together. This is one time in soccer when every player can use hands. You pass the ball to a teammate with a nice, easy toss (or, occasionally, a long throw). The only way that player can move the ball is by heading it. After it has been headed, the ball should be picked up by a teammate (or, if it's a bad header, a defender), then tossed again. Of course, all goals must be scored by headers, too!

7 Throw-ins

It may seem as if throw-ins are a minor part of soccer. But games are won and lost in many random ways, and good throw-ins go a long way toward determining how well or poorly a team attacks.

A player with a good, long throw-in—a "gun"—can make a difference. A strong throw is also one method of getting noticed by a coach during tryouts.

A legal throw-in is not easy to learn, but once you've got it down you'll never forget it. (Because it's a bit difficult, many leagues ban throw-ins for very young players. Others allow youngsters to throw the ball in any way they can. But by the time you're eight or nine years old, you should learn how to take a legal throw-in.)

For starters, a throw-in must originate behind the head. That means holding the ball with two hands, and bending the elbows as far as you can. Your hands should feel comfortable on the ball. Don't grasp it too hard, or too loosely.

Both feet must be on the ground when you throw. You can run up to the sideline, and even drag the toes of one foot behind you. But when the throw is taken, stay on the ground. No jumping allowed!

The throw should come in one complete motion, with no starting and stopping. The ball should come over the top of your head, not off to one side. That puts spin on the ball, and the ball should not spin. Both hands should hold the ball with equal strength.

When the ball is released, both hands should be extended in front of you, about head height. If you release too early, the ball will go high but not far. If you wait too long, the ball will drop right in front of you—and you're not allowed to touch it again until at least one other player has. You should follow through after you throw it: In other words, don't just release the ball and then stop. Keep your hands moving all the way down to your sides.

Then—and this is an important point—get yourself back on the field of play. Don't just pat yourself on the back for a good throw—get moving!

As far as where your throw should go, try not to throw to a teammate who is too close. Chances are that teammate's too near the sideline to handle it, or it won't have enough follow-through to be legal. On the other hand, you should not aim for a teammate who is too far away either. Long throws are the easiest to intercept. Try for a teammate who is a medium distance away. Aim for the ball to land at the feet or chest (or, if the teammate is a very good header, the head). A throw to any other part of the body is too hard to handle.

The best way to become a good thrower-in (or is it "throw-inner"?) is to practice with a friend. Start close; make sure the receiver is able to handle your throws like a soccer player (in other words, not just catching the ball with the hands!). As you get confident, increase the distance between you. Then add a defender, behind the receiver. The receiver should be "passive" at first (not trying to win the ball). Soon the receiver can become active, and attempt to win it. The final step is for the receiver to play the ball back to you, or keep it as the thrower comes back on the field. Either way, you and your friend have a 2-v.-1 against the defender. Attack a goal made out of cones. Try to score on it; then switch roles.

The Throw-in Game

This is a variation on the heading game described earlier. Divide your friends into two equal teams; if you've got low numbers, bring the goals in closer. You play the throw-in game just like regular soccer, with this exception: The only way to pass the ball is with a legal throw-in. Each throw-in should be controlled, dribbled once or twice, then picked up. The player picking up the ball then becomes the thrower. Of course, all goals must be scored with legal throw-ins, too. It's fun, it's good exercise—and it helps you develop that awesome throw that will one day win a game for your team!

8 Shielding and Screening

Once you've got the idea of ball control and dribbling down, you're ready for the next step: not losing the ball. You've worked hard to control it; now you want to be able to do something with it.

"Shielding" and "screening" are two terms that mean pretty much the same thing: using your body to protect the ball at all costs.

The basic principle behind shielding and screening is *keeping your body between your opponent and the ball*. It doesn't matter if you're the smallest player on the field; if your body comes between the other guy or girl and the ball, it's going to be very difficult for even the most humongous opponent to get it.

Shielding and screening takes place at a much slower pace than dribbling. The fewer touches you have on the ball, and the less you move, the greater the chance you won't make a mistake that results in giving up the ball. What you're trying to do is always keep yourself between the opponent and the ball. Every time he or she moves to win it, you make a countermove to keep the ball.

You should make your body as big as possible, by spreading your legs sideways as much as you can, while moving your arms away from your sides. You are not allowed to raise them high, or make contact with an opponent, but you can try to create space around you by moving your arms a bit.

At some point your opponent may commit to winning the ball (by moving hard to one side, for example). That's the point when you should make your countermove, by dribbling into space and out of danger. If you can't—if, let's say, you are too close to a sideline or end line—you can try knocking the ball right at your opponent, hoping it will ricochet out of bounds for a throw-in, goal kick, or corner kick.

It's not easy to practice shielding, but there are a couple of fun games you and your friends can try.

Give It a Ride, Part I

Use the center circle as your boundary. Everyone has a ball—except one player. Everyone with a ball tries to shield and screen it, while that one player tries to kick as many soccer balls as possible outside the circle. In the beginning, everyone with the ball will move slowly. However, the more you do this, the more confident you'll get. Soon you'll be dribbling away from your opponent, and will only have to use your shielding and screening skills at the last moment.

Give It a Ride, Part II

Once you've got that game down, try a variation. Every player has a ball, but the idea this time is to knock other players' soccer balls out of the circle while you're protecting your own. This means you've got to move quite a bit, look up, change direction—*and* keep your soccer ball under control. It's not easy, but you'll really get a "kick" out of it! (Ugh.)

9 **Tackling**

Like shielding and screening, "tackling" sounds like a tactic that's out of place here. Football, maybe. But what does "tackling" have to do with soccer?

Plenty. If you can't tackle, your team will hardly ever have the ball. And if you don't have the ball, you won't be able to execute all the other skills you've just learned.

"Tackling" is the art of winning the ball from an opponent. He or she has got it, and is dribbling along (or perhaps shielding and screening). You want it. So you tackle.

If this were football, you'd tackle using your hands. However, it's soccer, so you tackle with your feet.

The first thing you do is approach the ball. This is easiest when your opponent is moving

63

slowly, or not at all. That's why you want to first slow down the player, if possible.

Then bring your tackling foot back slightly, as if you were going to strike the ball with the inside of the foot. With your weight low—*way* low—swing the foot, and make contact with the ball, right about mid-center. Because your opponent is also making contact with the ball, there will be a loud *thwack*! That's the sound of your foot striking the ball, at the same time it is protected by your opponent's foot.

It should be a satisfying *thwack*! That means you've made good contact. Now, follow through. This means keeping your weight low, and moving forward even if the ball is momentarily stuck to the other player's foot. By following through, you're trying to drag the ball over his or her foot, or in some other way loosen it from that player's control. It's important to use your whole body to follow through—upper body strength helps win tackles. You're not pushing your opponent away, but you *are* using your body and technique to claim the ball.

Timing is important. If you try to tackle too early, you'll whiff and kick air. If you tackle too late, your opponent will already be gone. You need to be near enough to your opponent so you don't have to lunge, yet not so close that you can't lean over the ball (not leaning makes you a lot easier to knock over).

It is also important to tackle as if you mean it. If you don't put all your effort into a tackle, you won't win the ball. Don't be afraid of getting hurt: Almost all tackling injuries occur when a player goes in too lightly. Going in hard does not guarantee that you will win the ball, but it does lessen your chances of getting knocked off balance.

Once you've won a tackle, it is important to move quickly away. The player from whom you just stole the ball will not be very happy. So don't give your opponent a chance to try a tackle of his or her own. Dribble, pass, shoot—whatever you do, don't just stand there congratulating yourself for your great tackle!

Tackle Training

Stand a few inches away from a partner; put a ball in between. At the count of "3," you both try to tackle. This is a good way to practice timing, as well as keeping your weight low. The more tackles you try, the more you'll understand the importance of following through.

Once you get the feel—*thwack!*—of tackling, you and your friend can move farther apart. First take one step away; again, count to "3" and tackle. Then take another step away. Remember not to lunge, but instead, take a couple of quick steps to get to the ball.

Next, try tackling a player who is actually shielding and screening. Again, timing is as important as technique. You can't tackle when you don't see the ball; make sure you wait until the ball is near, then go for it.

Later, try tackling a player who is dribbling. This is harder, because the ball is moving. Don't get frustrated if you try to tackle and miss. Tackling is not easy to do, but the more you practice, the sharper you'll get.

After that, get a third friend to roll a ball between you and your other friend. Now you're trying to control a loose ball, tackle it away from an opponent who gets it first, or (if the ball arrives perfectly between you), win it with a tackle. As soon as you do, start on the fun part: Go to goal (two cones 20 yards away). Try to score—unless, that is, your friend manages to tackle the ball away from you first!

Finally, you can play a game (which also helps develop dribbling skills). Set up two "goal lines" 20–30 yards apart. You stand on one side, with a ball; your friend stands on the other side, without one. Your job is to dribble all the way across the other goal line. Your friend's job, of course, is to stop you—first by slowing you down, then by tackling away the ball. When a goal is scored, or the ball is tackled away, switch places. This is very game-related, because it teaches you how to slow down an opponent, wait for the right moment—then go for the ball with a goal behind you.

Steal the Bacon

Two teams of players line up 20 yards apart. Each team's player has a number. When a number is called, that player from each team races to the middle, and tries to win the one ball that is sitting there. Because most of the time the two players arrive at the same time, good tackling skills are necessary to gain control. The player who wins the ball then tries to dribble back over his or her own line. The other player, obviously, tries to stop this, which leads to even more tackling opportunities. Each time a player succeeds in getting back to his or her starting line, that player's team gets one point.

Four Grids

Set up four grids (squares), one in back of the other. Each grid is roughly 10 yards long and 10 yards wide. Set up four defenders: one on the back line of each grid. Then get several dribblers, each with a ball, to line up, one behind the other, ready to attack. The first dribbler enters the first grid; his job is to get past the defender, and into the second grid, without having the ball tackled away, or losing it with a poor touch. He does the same in the second, third, and fourth grids, trying to keep control to the end. As soon as Player A leaves the first grid, has the ball tackled away, or miskicks it, Player B enters. Defenders should start as close to the back line of each grid as possible. Things get very hectic, but everyone receives plenty of practice at ball control *and* tackling.

The next step is to add a second attacker, so that instead of going 1-v.-1, defenders are faced with 2-v.-1 situations.

Come Join Us

Six to eight attackers line up on the sideline, close—but not too close—together. Halfway across the field are two defenders. The object is for the attackers to dribble past the defenders, to the other sideline. The defenders should wait for the dribblers to come, and can only move laterally (side to side); they should not move forward against them. However, if they are beaten they may turn and pursue, trying to prevent an attacker from reaching the far sideline. When an attacker is tackled and loses the ball to a defender, he joins them for the next round, which begins from the opposite sideline. Slowly the number of defenders increases, and the number of attackers decreases. The attacker left at the end is the winner.

10 Goalkeeping

In a book about a sport where you don't use your hands, a whole section devoted to using your hands?

Yep.

Without goalkeepers (also called "keepers" or "goalies"), soccer just would not be the same. Trying to score on an empty net is too easy, and trying to defend the goal without a keeper behind you is too hard.

Goalkeeping is a special art, just like ball control or dribbling or shooting. It's an art that can be learned, even though some players have more of a natural talent and interest in it than others. But it's also an art that can wait. Most young teams do not

even have goalies; short-sided soccer is the way to start. When teams start playing full-field, they'll need a keeper. However, that does not mean they should have a "permanent" goalie. Until the age of 12 or 13, experts say, it's good to alternate several players in goal. That way one boy or girl does not feel too much pressure. In addition, different players get exposed to the position—and, because keepers get some time out in the field, they learn all the foot skills they'll soon need.

So don't be shy! Give goalie a try! It's fun to dive and fly! And that's no lie!

Strength and Agility

Three of the key qualities of any goalkeeper are agility (moving quickly and loosely), flexibility, and coordination. There are many ways to become more agile, flexible, and coordinated: for example, arching your back with just the soles of your feet and palms of your hand on the ground; jumping rope; stepping up and down quickly on two stairs; running side to side along a line (don't cross your feet); and trampolining (be careful!). Get in the goal mouth; practice moving side to side, and jumping high. Don't worry if you can't touch the crossbar at first; eventually you'll grow, and will be able to. Work on developing good technique first; the rest will follow.

Goalkeepers also need strength. Strong legs provide power for jumping, while a strong upper body enables you to withstand challenges in the air, grab a ball, and hold on to it. Any exercise that increases strength is good. Although you should not lift a lot of heavy weights until you reach puberty, doing repetitions (10–12 per set, three sets every other day) with low weights can help "prime" your body to become strong. Push-ups, with both hands on the ball, also help develop strength. But be sure to keep your back straight; don't bend at the waist.

Reflexes

Here's a great way to develop hand–eye coordination. Squat on the ground, a couple of feet away from a practice partner who stands, holding one soccer ball in each hand. Without giving any kind of hand, eye, or body signal, your partner suddenly drops one ball. Your job is to catch it before it hits the ground. Try to dive forward, "smothering" the ball by bringing it close to your chest.

Your partner will vary the timing between drops, so you really must concentrate well. As you get better at this, he or she can move a step or two away. This means you have to spring out a little farther to catch the ball. If your partner also lowers his or her arms, the ball does not have as far to drop—meaning you must react even quicker.

You can also "shadow" the movements of a friend who is running around the field. Every time your friend changes direction or speed, or puts on a feint, you do the same. You'll develop awesome powers of concentration, and soon be able to react even when the other person does not realize he or she is doing something different.

For extra fun, have a friend kick or throw footballs—yes, footballs!—on the ground in front of the goal. They take much stranger bounces than soccer balls. If you get in the habit of saving weirdly bouncing, oddly shaped footballs, you should have no problem at all when you're attacked by perfectly round soccer balls!

Diving

As mentioned above, diving is an important part of goal-keeping. You can practice diving by sitting with your legs spread apart. Your friend starts by kicking or rolling the ball: first to one side, then the other, then alternating. (Your friend should have several balls at his or her side, so if you miss one the drill can continue.)

Your dive is simply extending your body sideways. The first thing that should hit the ground is the ball (clutched in your hands), followed by your forearm, shoulder, side, hip, thigh, legs, and feet.

When you've got the hang of it, your friend can start striking balls a little farther away. Now you're extending yourself more, learning to "reach" for balls. As soon as your fingertips make contact with the ball, bring it as close in as

you can. Soon, you can squat instead of sit. Now you will spring sideways for the ball, instead of simply falling on it. You're learning to keep your weight low—an important trait for all goalies as they move side to side in the net.

Finally, add an obstacle that you must dive over. Start with something soft, like a blanket or sweatshirt. Then make it harder, bulkier, or bigger—say, a bag filled with balls. This forces you to really *spring* to the side. (To get extra power and extension, take one or two shuffle steps before diving. But be careful not to cross one leg in front of the other—that's a sure way to fall down and tangle yourself up.)

Catching Low Balls

Low balls seem deceptively easy to catch. However, at one time or another every keeper in the world has let an easy shot roll through her legs. The reason is usually carelessness. Taking your eye off the ball—even for a split second—can make you unprepared if the ball takes a weird bounce. Sometimes, unless you look, you don't even realize you have not bent down far enough.

When catching low balls, keep your feet close together (this helps prevent shots from rolling through). Lean forward at the waist. Hold your hands slightly apart; your palms should face the ball, and your fingertips should almost touch the ground. Let the ball roll up your palms and forearms, then bring it in to your chest.

It is *not* a good idea to go down on one knee. This does not allow you to move easily in case of a bad bounce; it also slows your release of the ball, since you must stand up before making your outlet pass.

Catching Waist and Chest Balls

To catch a ball aimed at your stomach, bend slightly forward but keep your arms pressed tightly against your ribs. Your palms should face outward. Your hands make the first contact with the soccer ball, but then you quickly absorb the impact by taking a slight backward step. (So don't stand on your line to save shots. If you step backward, you'll bring the ball across the goal line—and it will count as a goal.)

To catch a ball aimed at your chest, hold your elbows slightly in front of your chest; your palms should be slightly out, and slightly down. As soon as the ball hits your hands, bring it in toward your chest.

You'll need a partner to practice these saves. A partner can toss the ball to you, underhand or overhand, gradually increasing the distance and power of the throws. He or she can also kick or bounce passes to you; these are more difficult to handle, because they are not as accurately aimed, and you have less time to judge where they are heading.

Catching and Punching High Balls

To catch head-high balls, form a diamond with your hands. As soon as you make contact with the ball, bring it in toward your chest. It's just like catching a baseball or football (only bigger). You've got to watch the ball all the way into your hands, and you should "give" as soon as the ball hits you (no stiff hands).

To catch high balls, push off the ground with one foot. As you leap in the air, bring the other foot up toward your chest. This carries you higher. Raise both hands high, with your fingers spread wide. When your fingertips touch the ball, bring it down into your chest. Hold it there. Congratulations on your save—the ball is yours! No one on the field can do anything until you get rid of it, so wait until you're good and ready to release it.

Sometimes a ball is so high you can't catch it, but you can get your fingertips on it. In this case, you'll have to punch it out of danger. If you've got the whole field in front of you, make fists with your two hands, bring them together, and use a two-fisted punch. Keep in mind that the ball should go "high and wide." Punch it hard, and punch it to the outside of the field. If you punch it short, or in the middle—across the goal mouth—it might come right back at you. (The last thing you want is to see that darn ball again soon.)

If the ball is too difficult to catch or even punch away, you should try to tip it over the top of the crossbar. Jumping high and using the back of your hand, flick the ball over the end line. Sure, you've given up a corner kick—but you have also saved a goal.

To practice catching high balls, find a partner who is tall, and ask a third person to throw (or, if she is accurate, kick) high balls. At first, simply jump over your partner as she stands in front of you, and make the catch. Later she can jump as you do, forming an obstacle in front. Then she can attempt to head the ball at the same time you try to catch it. If she is really creative, she will jump at the *wrong* time, forcing you to make a decision about the best time to leap in order to catch the ball at its height.

How can you practice catching if you don't have a partner? A good drill begins as you lie on your back. Toss the ball in the air; catch it, then bring it down to your chest. Sound easy? It is—until you try doing it with your eyes closed. The idea here is to develop a sensitive "feel" for the ball. If you do this over and over, many times a day, catching becomes almost automatic; it is something you feel confident doing even if you can't see the ball (which sometimes happens in matches).

Another exercise has you sitting on the ground, with a ball in your hand. Kick it high in the air; spring up quickly; and catch the ball before it hits the ground. This also develops your foot skills—the more accurate your kick, the greater the chance you'll get to it. For a special challenge, try to leap up without using your hands!

One final goalkeeping point to keep in mind: As a goalkeeper, you have a tremendous advantage over everyone else on the field, because you can use your hands. This gives you an extension of about a foot over other players. However, every time you don't jump, you give up that advantage. So practice getting off the ground—and get those hands high in the air!

High-Low

After working on catching and punching, you and a friend can play high-low. Your friend (who has a good supply of soccer balls) alternates serving low balls that you've got to dive for, and high ones that you must catch or punch. Your friend also alternates side to side, so that all the low balls come on one side, all the high ones on the other. After a couple of minutes, switch sides. In the beginning, your friend should wait until you're ready before serving each ball. When you've got the hang of it, your friend can start serving each ball as soon as you've made the previous save.

Circle Shots

When you've mastered saving high and low, you're ready to see some real shots. Your teammates can take their places on the outside of the center circle, each with a ball. You, of course, crouch in a ready position in the middle. When someone—you, a teammate, or the coach—says "Go!" the first person shoots on you. After you've saved and passed the ball back to the shooter (or gotten up after a miss), the next person shoots. Keep going in a predetermined direction, clockwise or counterclockwise. Players on the outside should be alert for shots that are too wide, or that slip underneath you. The idea is to keep the balls at the feet of the players in the circle; if too many go too high or wide (or you make 10 saves in a row), the exercise ends. (A reminder to shooters: Do not strike stationary balls. It's important to give the ball a little push forward before shooting. This makes the exercise a bit more game related.)

The next step is to take random shots. You'll need someone to shout out the name of each shooter, in no particular order: "Brad!" "Tyler!" "Lizzie!" "Alex!" Obviously, this is a lot harder for the keeper. Spend a few minutes studying where everyone is before the shooting starts—and keep your weight low, so you can shift quickly from one shooter to the next. As before, the better you become, the faster the caller can call the shots.

Shooting on Goal

Remember the shooting exercises we talked about earlier? They're just as important for the keeper. But they can be adapted specially for the goalie, too. They're just like the circle shots, except this time when the players shoot, either in order or randomly, they're lined up 10–15 yards from the goal. (Of course, they should push the ball forward, and hit a moving—not stationary—ball.) Now you've got something to protect, so this becomes a keeper drill. And because you're so awesome at intimidating the shooters, just watch as the shots fly high and wide—anywhere but into the net.

Outlets

The keeper's final task, once she has saved a goal, is to "outlet" (throw or kick) the ball to a teammate. Throws can be made several ways: rolling it along the ground to a nearby player, cupping the ball between the palm and forearm and throwing sidearm to someone reasonably close, or whipping it overhead like a baseball to a teammate fairly far away.

Kicks can be regular punts (dropped onto the laces, then belted far), or half-volleys (dropped on the ground, then struck just as they start to bounce up). Be sure to follow through with your entire body, even adding a little hop-skip after striking the ball if you can. This adds power to your kicks.

Keepers also should become adept at taking goal kicks. Earlier we talked about the proper way to kick the ball. For goal kicks, where distance is important, you'll want to lean back and strike slightly underneath the center. Again, follow-through is crucial.

The best way to get good at outlets is to practice. Ask a friend to stand at certain parts of the field; begin throwing and kicking, and see what works best. You should learn to outlet the ball several different ways, but of course you'll develop your own particular style. Just make sure your friend is moving; you always want your teammates to be in motion when they get the ball. Soccer players don't stand still!

Game-Related Situations

The best way to practice goalkeeping is to put yourself in game-related situations. Small-sided games do this in a big way. For example, you and several friends can play 3-v.-3 or 4-v.-4. The difference between this and other short-sided games is that you are playing in an actual goal.

How does this work? It's entirely up to you. One way is for both teams to shoot on you after completing, say, three or five passes in a row. (If you save a shot or they miss, the count goes back to zero.) You'll see plenty of shots this way, and get a chance to work on other aspects of your game such as positioning.

You can design any small-sided game to work on whatever weakness you might have. Let's imagine you need work on crosses. Set up a small-sided game in which both teams fire on you, but they can shoot only after a cross has been made. This ensures you won't get battered to death, while at the same time giving you plenty of practice saving crosses in a relatively short amount of time.

Penalty Kicks

Every goalkeeper worries about penalty kicks. In fact, the real pressure is on the shooter. He's supposed to make the shot; you're not expected to save it.

But if you can, that's great. The best advice we can give you is to relax. Keep your body weight low, and be ready to move the instant the ball is kicked. Try to read clues in the shooter's approach, to determine which side he will shoot at. Some shooters look directly at the corner they're aiming for (of course, others do this as a decoy; then they fire at the opposite corner!). Some shooters turn their hips in the direction of the shot, just before striking the ball. Others go to the same side all the time, so it helps to remember where a particular kicker shot the last time he took a penalty kick.

Once you've made your decision, don't second-guess yourself. Extend your body as far as you can, try to get a hand on the ball, and listen for your teammates' roar. All you can do is give it your best, um, "shot," and hope for the best possible outcome.

11 Warming Up

When you're young—say, five years old—you can run onto the field and start running and kicking without any kind of warm-up. But as you get older—say, at seven years old—it's a good idea to warm up first. Even if the weather is broiling, your body still needs a chance to "get warm." And a warmed-up soccer player plays better than a cool one.

A good warm-up takes 10 minutes up to age 12, and about 15 minutes for teenagers. It should involve everything you will do during a game, except tackling and heading.

Many players like to start with a short run, moving back and forth across the field with the ball at their feet. Then comes stretching, working from top to bottom (neck to ankles), or bottom to top. Do each stretch at least three times, and hold each stretch for 5–10 seconds—long enough to feel the muscles stretching, but not to the point of pain. (Remember, don't "bounce" while stretching. Just s-t-r-e-t-c-h your muscles out—hold them there—and gradually increase the stretch each *time* you do it, not *during* the stretch.)

Here are a few good stretches:

◉ **Calf and lower leg:** Get in a poor push-up position: hands on the ground, but butt way up in the air. Then keep one foot flat on the ground, but relax the other as if you were about to start a race. You should feel the stretch in your calf and lower leg.

◉ **Hamstring (back of the thigh):** Lying flat on your back, cup both hands around the back of your knee; bend your knee slightly, and pull your leg slowly toward your head. Keep the opposite knee flat on the ground. Make sure you stretch the hamstrings on both legs!

Another hamstring stretch: While standing up, with legs straight or slightly bent, cross one foot over the other. Slowly bend over, until you feel the muscle stretch in the back of your leg.

Also: Stand, and spread your legs far apart. Slowly bend at the waist to one side; touch your toes, if possible. After 10 seconds, bend to the other side. Then cross your arms in front of you, bend at the waist, and bring your arms as far to the ground as possible.

Also: Sit down, and spread your legs apart slightly wider than your shoulders. Reach forward slowly, and try to touch your toes. Keep your head bent slightly forward.

⚽ **Quadriceps (front of the thigh):** While standing, grab the top of one foot with the hand on the same side. Slowly pull the foot up to your butt, until you feel your quadricep muscle stretching. Hold for 10–15 seconds. Alternate legs, and repeat.

⚽ **Hip:** Stand on one leg. Lift the opposite leg off the ground, then slowly swing it open (to the side). Just as slowly swing it shut (to the center of your body), and lower it to the ground. Your arms should be extended to the sides, to keep your balance. Do not twist your body; keep it facing forward. Then switch legs, and repeat.

⚽ **Gluteus (butt muscle):** Sit on the ground. Keeping your back straight, wrap one hand around the opposite knee and pull that knee toward your chest. The foot should cross over the opposite thigh, and the toes of that foot should point outward. The bottom of the foot that is extended straight out should rest on the ground, for balance. After holding that position for a few seconds, twist your upper body. Then switch legs, and repeat.

⚽ **Groin:** Sit on the ground, with your back straight and your feet spread so that your heels and the bottom of your feet are touching each other. Hold your ankles with your hands. Using your elbows, push down on the insides of your thighs.

Also: Squat down, and extend one leg to the side. As the knee of the extended leg straightens, the inside of the thigh begins to stretch.

⚽ **Lower back:** Lie face down. With your palms flat on the ground, push your upper body up as far as you can without feeling pain. Keep your legs together, and your eyes staring straight ahead (not up).

⚽ **Upper body:** Standing straight up, hold both arms together over your head (clasp your fingers together). Keeping your arms straight, lean to one side—far enough to feel your muscles stretch. Then stretch to the other side; then forward, and back.

⚽ **Neck:** Drape one hand over the top of your head, so that the palm is pressed against the opposite side of your head. Pull your head gently downward. Then switch sides, and repeat.

After stretching you can run a bit, this time without the ball. Sprint forward; also run backward and sideways.

Then grab a ball, and pass it around in groups of two or three. You can knock around a series of short passes, or play low-pressure keepaway. You might juggle, by yourself or with a small group. You could go over a few moves you've been working on. If you'll be hitting long passes during a game, try some of those with a partner. If you normally take throw-ins, corner kicks, or goal kicks, practice some of those, too. (This not only gets you in the groove, it also helps you figure out game-related things like which way the wind is blowing, and how wide the field is.)

The better your warm-up, the better you'll play once the game or practice begins. With a good warm-up, you're not doing things for the first time under game or training pressure. You've already done them with no pressure, so your body is relaxed and ready.

Warm-up is not a time to tire yourself out or compete with teammates. It is simply a time to get loose, relax, and prepare for the game or practice ahead.

12 Cooling Down

One of the most neglected parts of soccer is the cooldown. Just like the warm-up, this prepares your body—in this case, your muscles and mind get ready to rest. Spending 5 or 10 minutes after a game or practice cooling down—stretching, perhaps jogging lightly—helps prevent muscle fatigue later that day, and ensures that you wake up feeling fresh the next morning. It might seem silly to stretch and jog lightly *after* you've just run and kicked hard for over an hour, but don't knock it until you've tried it!

Some teams jog across the field together (you need to go across and back two or three times; once just isn't enough). This is a time for chatting, laughter, and waving to the fans if you've won. If you've lost, you can talk about the shot that would have gone in if it hadn't hit the crossbar, or make a vow that the next time those other guys are *definitely* goin' down.

After your cooldown jog, you can gather in a circle and stretch together. This is a lot less formal than your pregame stretching, but it's just as important. In addition to preventing tightness and cramps, it allows you a few extra minutes before having to endure well-meaning but silly questions from parents, grandparents, and friends about why you missed that shot from so close in (Didn't they notice the three defenders all around you?). Or how could the ref have missed that penalty kick (Well, it was actually three feet *outside* the box).

Of course, there's one cooldown that's the most fun of all: parading around a stadium holding a trophy over your head. That's the ultimate dream of any soccer player. And the more you practice these 20 steps (including the all-important cooldown), the greater your chance of being able to do exactly that.

13 Physical Fitness

Everyone knows that soccer is a running game. Professional players run six or eight miles in a game. That sounds like a lot (and it is!), but there is more. Soccer involves almost constant stop-and-go running—quick sprints over short distances—so players need not only stamina but acceleration, too.

That's great if you're a natural-born runner. But what if you're not?

Most of us aren't. That does not mean we should hang up our boots. There are plenty of ways to develop running skills, both short and long distance. If your genes haven't programmed you for it, you may never be the quickest player on the team, but with a little effort and training, you can sure be a lot faster than you are now.

Acceleration

The next time you watch a soccer game, take your eye off the ball. Focus on the players who are *not* dribbling or kicking. Watch how they run. Notice the defender who gets beaten, turns, and races back 5 or 10 yards to try to win the ball back. Check out the teammate who makes a 10- or 15-yard overlapping run in order to receive a pass. Even the goalkeeper runs, sprinting from one side of the box to the other in order to get in the best position for a shot that may never come.

The key to covering a short distance as rapidly as possible is acceleration. In car talk, that means going from 0 to 60; in soccer talk it's probably 0 to 10. Acceleration in people is a combination of reflexes and power. It's also technique: Short steps are better than long ones, and the lower you keep your weight, the easier it is to blast away.

It's best to practice acceleration with a friend—that way you've got someone with whom to compete and measure progress. Draw a line or set a cone 5 to 10 yards away. On a third person's command (that way there's no cheating), burst forward toward the "goal." Remember to stay low: you're creating more power, and there is less resistance.

After a few quick races, start from a different position: lying on your stomach. Now you've got to scramble up, and accelerate from there. Then try other positions: lying on your back; sitting with your legs crossed; sitting with your back to the ball; kneeling. In soccer, you're often forced to accelerate from an awkward starting point, so this is all good practice—and fun.

Another excellent acceleration drill is to jog 15 yards, run 15 more yards at three-quarter speed, then sprint the final 15. After crossing the "finish line," gradually slow to a jog. Rest; then repeat several more times. Make sure that each of the three segments is run at a distinctly different speed.

Stop-and-Gos

Now it's time to add some changes of direction to your acceleration. After all, most running in soccer is *not* done in a straight line.

Set cones 10–15 yards away. Plan in advance how many times you and a friend will race back and forth. Each time you turn—at the cone or the starting line—make sure to lean down and touch the ground. This keeps your body as low as possible.

When you get good at this, add a ball. It's important to learn to run while dribbling—and stopping the ball dead on the line is a skill everyone needs.

Follow the Leader

Many times, running with a friend helps you train faster, longer, and harder. But instead of simply jogging, or even sprinting, together, try Follow the Leader. Your friend runs in random fashion around a large area. You follow a couple of yards behind. However, he or she constantly changes speed and direction. You'll be amazed at how much distance you cover—and how hard you work.

Go Fetch

A good way to break up the monotony of running is to have a ball. Dribble out 15, 20, 30 yards—any distance, really—and back. Stop the ball as close to yourself as possible each time you turn. For variety, dribble out with the ball; leave it; run back to your starting line; go fetch it; and dribble it back in. You can also do this as a race against your friend. If you've got even numbers greater than two, team up: One person dribbles out, leaves the ball, runs back; then the next person runs out, collects the ball, and dribbles home. Other possibilities are limited only by your imagination.

Another Go Fetch exercise works at the same time on shooting accuracy. Start in the center circle. Kick the ball as far downfield as possible; then sprint after it. As soon as you catch up to your own "pass," fire a shot on goal. If you score, jog to the net, fetch the ball, then jog back to the center circle and repeat. If you miss, *sprint* to retrieve the ball, then jog back to the center circle, and repeat. (You reward yourself for scoring by not having to sprint a second time!)

Stamina

In addition to short- and middle-distance running—which you're developing in the exercises above—you can work on long distances, too. This gives you the lung and leg power to cover those six or eight miles the pros do (or whatever the equivalent is on a smaller field!).

Interval running is a great way to build stamina. It's not easy, but the results are worth it. Set cones at varying distances: 20 yards, 40, 60 (midfield). The idea is to run, at about three-quarter speed, out and back. The amount of time you spend resting at the starting line should be equal to the amount of time you spend running out and back. At first, start low: out-and-back 20 yards, rest, repeated three times. Then go out-and-back 40 yards, rest, repeated three times. Do the same to midfield. Then start decreasing the distance: out-and-back 40 yards, rest, repeated three times. And, finally, 20 yards, out-and-back, repeated three times.

As you build stamina—a process that may take several weeks—you can increase the number of repetitions. If you are breathing hard, that's good. It is important, however, not to lean forward, with your hands on your knees, when you rest between runs. That compresses your lungs, and prevents you from getting lots of air into your lungs. Instead, stand up tall, put your hands behind your head, and breathe deeply. This helps train your body to use oxygen efficiently.

Another way to build stamina is by running a buildup, around the outside of the field. Divide the field into six parts: each end line is one (for a total of two); each sideline is two, divided by midfield (for a total of four). Start by sprinting one section, from the corner of the end line to midfield; then slowly jog one section. Next, sprint two sections; then jog one. Then sprint three and jog one. Now start back down: sprint two, jog one; sprint one, jog one.

Gradually, work yourself up to the point where you can sprint the entire field—all six sections—and then start back down again.

These are, of course, just guidelines. You can adapt your buildup to your particular age and fitness level. Perhaps it's easier to jog two sections in between each sprint. Find out what works best for you. And don't try to do too much too soon.

For variety's sake, you can also vary your runs—sometimes jogging the sidelines, and sprinting diagonally across the field; other times looping your runs behind the goal, in a figure eight.

Don't neglect your lateral (sideways) and backward running, either. You don't have to do a lot of this, but if you train yourself to become quicker in all directions, you'll be even more valuable than if you can only run fast while going forward. (Note: When running laterally, take small, quick steps, but do not cross one foot over the other. When running backward, take similar small steps—and keep glancing over your shoulder to see where you're going!)

You should not do distance work every day. Alternate your short-distance training (acceleration, stop-and-gos) with your long-distance work. That way you don't get burned out mentally—and your body stays fresh physically.

Don't forget to run hills. These are not easy, but the resistance they provide is excellent. And don't think that coming down is easy—running *downhill* is sometimes more difficult than running uphill, because you're "braking" with muscles you don't often use.

You can use a soccer ball to develop fitness, too, of course. Slalom dribbling—dribbling through six or eight cones, each about 3 yards apart—is excellent, especially if you do three sets before resting. Then do three more sets— and rest—before finishing off with another set!

Also great for stamina are 1-v.-1 games, particularly when you work hard for a minute at a time. You can play simple keepaway—trying to keep the ball from your opponent, while always moving—or go 1-v.-1 with a "goal" (one cone that you both try to knock over, or two goals 20 yards apart). The important thing is to keep moving the entire time. After a minute rest (you deserve it!), go 1-v.-1 again. And again, and again, and again. . . .

Another good fitness drill is called Catch Me If You Can. Two players jog in the center circle; one has a ball, the other doesn't. Suddenly, the player with the ball begins dribbling for one of the two goals, at either end of the field (a smart player will pick the right time to do this, when the other person is momentarily distracted or a few feet away). The player without the ball must race after the other, and try to prevent him or her from getting off a shot on the open goal. Give a point for each goal scored. After a few times doing this—alternating, of course—you'll understand why all soccer players must be in excellent shape!

Leg Power

Constant kicking and running helps develop strong legs. Most soccer players don't need to do anything special to build up their lower body. But some want to add even more power. There are four ways to do this.

1. One is through toe raises, which develops your calves. Toe raises are as easy as they sound. Simply stand in one spot, and raise yourself up on all toes. Repeat 10, 20, 50 times—it's up to you. You can do this anywhere, any time (within limits—your teacher might not like it if you start doing toe raises in the middle of class!).

2. Another method for developing leg strength is step-ups. You can use any surface that is slightly higher than the one you're on now (provided it's sturdy!). Alternating feet, step up onto the surface, then down. Make sure you really *raise* your foot, rather than just slapping it lazily down.

3. A third way is by jumping. Since jumping for jumping's sake seems silly, add in some heading practice. Ask a friend to hold a ball a few inches above your head. Practice jump-ing up, arching back, and heading the ball out of his hands. The better you get, the higher your friend can raise the ball. Just think: You're becoming a stronger header *and* developing more powerful leg muscles at the same time!

4. The final method is with wall squats. Stand with your back flat against a wall. Slowly squat down, until your hips are even with your knees. Hold for as long as you can without pain. If you get really strong, you can place a heavy book on your thighs as you squat. This is a great way to develop strong quadriceps (the muscles in your upper legs). Best of all, you can do it while watching your favorite TV show!

Upper Body Strength

Although soccer players are known for their lower body strength, it doesn't hurt to develop your upper body (abs and chest), too. Upper body strength helps you win tackles; adds distance to your throws; and makes you feel better, too.

You can develop your abs (abdominal muscles) by doing leg throws. Huh?! You'll see! Start by lying on your back, with a friend standing with his legs spread on either side of your shoulders. Slowly bring up your feet 90 degrees, so they point to the sky. Your friend then grabs your ankles and "throws" them back to the ground. Now comes the hard part: Use your abs to stop your feet just before they hit the grass. Ah . . . you feel it, right? Repeat as many times as you can stand it; then switch places and enjoy watching your friend groan as he builds up his own abs!

"Crunches" are good upper-body exercises, too. Lie on your back, but this time bend your knees. Now, with your elbows crossed over your chest, "crunch" your body forward, toward your knees. Repeat for 30–60 seconds. When you are "crunching," good form is more important than the number of crunches. If you "throw" yourself forward, you run the risk of injuring your back. Crunch s-l-o-w-l-y—and smoothly.

For a true "soccer-related" crunch, lie flat on your back with your arms behind your head, and the ball tucked between your ankles. Slowly raise your legs, arms, and back to a "V" position, then slowly lower them again—all without dropping the ball.

Another upper body exercise that involves the ball begins with you and a friend facing each other, and getting into push-up position—with your hands on a ball, instead of on the ground. By pushing and pulling on your soccer ball, try to knock your friend off balance. You can also use one ball and, facing each other, from a kneeling position with your arms wrapped around the ball, try to gain sole possession of it.

Flexibility

Flexibility is another important element of fitness. You can become more flexible by stretching. Whenever you stretch, begin with one part of the body and work to the other—in other words, head, neck, and shoulders on down to your ankles, or from bottom to top. Never "bounce"; instead, hold a stretch for 5–10 seconds at a time. And when you stretch, don't overdo it. You should feel your muscles stretching, but they should not hurt.

Over time, as you stretch each day, you will become more flexible. You will be able to touch the ground with your fingertips—perhaps even your palms. As you sit on the ground with your legs outstretched, you will lean forward and touch your toes—or beyond. Standing and bracing with one hand against a wall, you will bring one foot up to your butt higher than you ever could before.

Another good flexibility exercise is "bowling." (Isn't it amazing how many other sports are related to soccer?!) Holding a soccer ball on one sideline, bend over and "bowl" it forward 5–10 yards. Run after it; then reach down, pick it up, and bowl with the other hand. Repeat until you reach the other sideline.

The next time, play catch with yourself: Throw the ball up, leap to catch it at its highest point, then repeat all the way across and back.

The third time, alternate the two activities: first bowl, then throw and catch. After a few times, you'll feel as limber as a cat.

Other ideas include jumping with both feet from side to side over the ball; hopping over it from back to front, then back again; standing behind a ball and quickly lifting your feet, tapping it gently on the top in a quick, alternating rhythm; standing up, throwing the ball high, squatting down, then quickly getting up to catch it before it hits the ground.

How will all this help you become a better soccer player? The more flexible you are, the more things you can do with a ball—and with all parts of your body. The more flexible you are, too, the better able you are to resist injury. And we've never yet seen a soccer player who performed well while sitting on the sidelines, out with an injury!

Circuit Training

Circuit training combines many different types of physical fitness. Because you are constantly moving from one "station" to another, you don't get bored; at the same time, you are working different sets of muscles. You can design any type of "circuit" you want: for example, push-ups, jump rope, crunches, hopping through tires, juggling and dribbling between cones, pushing the ball forward and racing around a flag, passing the ball underneath a bench and then jumping over it to fetch it. Whatever you think of, you can do. Keep track of times, number of juggles, etc. Compete against yourself, or with friends.

14 Tactics and Concepts

You can't really practice tactics by yourself. Sometimes it's hard even to work on them with a friend. But we're mentioning a few key ideas here anyway. If you study them (maybe even print out some posters about them, to hang in your room), and make them a part of your game, you'll take a giant step on the road to becoming a good soccer player. Remember, soccer is not only about running, passing, shooting, and defending; it's also a game of thinking and creating. So think about these concepts:

☻ Soccer is a game of numbers. Sure, you start out evenly—11 against 11 for a full-size goal, 4-v.-4, 5-v.-5, or 6-v.-6 for short-sided games—but the idea is to get *numbers up* as often as possible. You want to create as many 2-v.-1 and 3-v.-2 situations as possible. The best way to do that is for all players to realize they are both . . .

☻ . . . Attackers and defenders. It does not matter whether you are a striker or a defender; when your team has possession, you are an attacker. And whether you're the furthest player back, or the first man forward, when the other team wins the ball you become a defender. This does not mean you race up and down the field like the Energizer bunny; that's the surest way to tire yourself out and *never* produce anything worthwhile. What it does mean is that *you think of yourself as an attacker and a defender,* and develop skills in both areas.

⚽ Generally, as soon as your team loses possession—no matter where on the field it happens—you should make the switch to defense. And you should make that transition in two ways: mentally (think "I'm a defender!") and physically (look around to see how you can help, then race to get into the proper defensive position). Similarly, the moment your team gains possession, you should switch again to an attacking mentality. Again, that means first thinking of yourself as an attacker, then looking up, and moving into whatever space will help your team attack. (Note: Moving forward is not always the best offensive idea. Attackers always need support "square" [to the side] and behind. Besides, if everyone always went forward, there would be no one back to help defensively once your team lost the ball.)

⚽ *Support,* which we just talked about, is *so* important. If a teammate has the ball, you should be supporting her. If you are close, this means getting in good position to receive a pass. Sometimes this support is forward or to the side (lateral); sometimes it is behind, for a "back pass." Alternatively, you can make a "dummy run" that takes a defender with you, opening up space into which your teammate can dribble. If you are not nearby, you can still support—perhaps by looking to get open one or two passes later, or staying back to help out on defense if your team suddenly loses the ball. If your team is not in possession, you can support by marking an opponent so he or she does not receive a pass, or perhaps "doubling up" (playing 2-v.-1) against an opponent who does have the ball. The important principle here involves not *what* you do but the fact that you provide some kind of support at all times on the field.

⚽ *Communication* is just as important as support. Soccer is a game of constant talk—but be sure you're saying something meaningful. "Yeah!" and "What you see" are not real helpful; "Go forward!" is. So are other directional signals: "You got me back!" "I'm square" (to the side). "Turn and burn!" (turn around, then sprint to goal). You can warn a teammate that an opponent is near; the universal call is "Man on!" even if the man is a girl. If no one is close, the correct (although ungrammatical) call is "You got time!" When a high ball is coming to a teammate, you can yell "Clear!" meaning he or she should head it out of danger. Whatever you say, be sure to say it loudly, clearly, and commandingly. Be certain everyone in the stands can hear your call. And don't be afraid of saying the wrong thing. The only way you learn how to talk on the field is by talking on the field.

⚽ The key defensive principle is to always be *goal side*— this means getting your body between the opponent and the goal. No matter what size you are, getting yourself in this position presents an obstacle, and either slows the opponent's path to the goal, or forces him or her outside. If you are beaten by an opponent, sprint back in as direct a path as possible to get goal side. Once there, be patient. Wait. Don't jump or lunge. Keep your weight low, with one leg slightly in front of the other (forcing your opponent to go to the outside, rather than straight at goal). Keep your eye on the ball; don't look at the other player's feet, or you might get tricked. Hold your arms away from your body; this gives you balance, and also provides more of an obstacle for your opponent to get around. The longer you "contain" (hold) your opponent, the less chance there is that she will be able to dribble forward, pass off, or shoot. The longer one holds the ball, the greater the chance one will make a mistake. And the longer you contain, the greater the chance your teammates will race back on defense to help you out.

⚽ There are two types of defense: man-to-man, and zone. Man-to-man defense (and, like "Man on!" the term is used even with females—go figure) requires tight marking of one opposing player. This means that when your team is defending, you follow one person wherever he goes. In zone defense, you are responsible not for a specific person, but rather a specific area of the field. You pick attackers up as they enter your area, then give them off to a teammate as they leave. Your coach will tell you which type of defense to play, depending upon his or her preferences, your team's strengths and weaknesses, and the opponents you face. In reality, most teams play a combination of man-to-man and zone, so there is tight marking at certain times (especially in dangerous situations in front of the goal), and looser marking at others.

⚽ Quick counterattacks are good—but not if they lose the ball. When your team wins the ball, especially on defense or at midfield, it's great to want to push forward quickly. But if no one is there—if everyone is back on defense, if your teammates are slow making the transition to attack, or if the other team has packed its own defense—then banging the ball upfield can be no different than handing it right back to the other team. There is a time for counterattacking, and a time for patience. Good players look up as soon as they win the ball. If the counterattack is there, they take it; if it is not, they hold on ("possess"), and wait for an attack to build. That's one more reason why the ability to control the ball (see "Shielding and Screening") is so important.

⚽ When taking corner kicks, do not aim too close to the goal. Corner kickers like to try to sneak one past the keeper, but that's extremely difficult. By serving a ball away from the keeper, you create more opportunities for shots—and also force the keeper to come out and commit to a save, opening up the goal for you and your teammates.

⚽ Direct and indirect kicks should not be wasted. Stay away from trick plays. Instead, examine the defensive setup for open areas to exploit, either in the wall or near it. Blasting a shot seldom works. If you can take a quick kick because the defenders are not set up, do so—but only if your teammates are ready. If the defenders have a good wall, take your time. Don't rush things. If the wall is too close, ask for 10 yards (but remember, if you ask the official for 10, you cannot begin play until he or she signals it is okay).

⚽ Penalty kicks are scary! There is a tremendous amount of pressure on one lonely kicker. Practice does not make perfect, but it sure improves the chances you'll make your "p.k." When practicing, pick one side— then always go there. The spot you choose should be low, and to the corner. Strike the ball hard, but don't kill it. If you take enough penalties, you'll be able to hit the same shot all the time. Then, when you come to the line, just visualize all the penalty kicks you've made in practice. "See" your foot strike the ball, and "watch it" as it sails, low and hard, into your favorite corner. Then do it! This is called "visualization," and believe it or not, it works!

15 Mental Preparation

Soccer is a physical game—ask anyone who's ever tried to run and kick and defend for an entire match!—but it is also a mental game. It's very important to start every game, even every practice, with a positive attitude. If you believe you're going to play well—that you can attack and defend, that you will support your teammates and in turn be supported by them, that you may not always make the right play but you sure as heck won't let your mistakes get you down—then you *will* play well.

If, on the other hand (er, foot), you start out with a negative attitude—worrying that the other team is better, bigger, or faster; that you'll choke if you ever get near the goal, even for a penalty kick; that because you let in a bad goal last game you'll do the same again this time—then you *will* play poorly.

Fortunately, with a little mental preparation, you can turn your negatives into positives. So far we've discussed physical drills, exercises, and games you can work on to play good soccer. Now it's time to focus on a few mental concepts.

And "focus" is certainly the right word, because that's where mental preparation begins. If you're not focused on soccer when you should be—during training and games—

then you won't be the best player you can be. (Focus works for everything else, too, by the way: playing piano, learning math, even being a good friend.) You don't have to be a 24–7, posters-on-the-wall, my-screen-name-is-Mia soccer fanatic, but you *do* have to give your full attention to the game when you're out on the field practicing or playing.

So don't let your mind wander. Don't think about the fight you just had with your brother, tomorrow's test in school, or even the stupid hat your coach is wearing. The time you spend on soccer should be enjoyable. Try not to let distractions drag you away from that joy.

During training, listen to instructions. Think about what you're supposed to be doing, and then do it as best you can. If you're confused, don't be afraid to ask questions, or look around to see what other players are doing. If one of your exercises involves dribbling a certain distance, dribble all the way. If one day you're supposed to work on your weak foot, then work on your weak foot. Don't settle for less than your best. The saying "You play the way you practice" may be old, but it's true. If you're satisfied with going halfway during training, then you'll do the same in a game. (Think about this, too: You'll be going halfway without using all the skills and moves you might possess had you gone a little bit harder during training!)

Preparing for a match is never easy, especially if your opponents really *are* better, bigger, and faster. It happens. But you know what? Every game starts with the same score: 0–0. It's an even contest until one side *proves* it's better. Don't put yourself or your team down. Keep in mind that you and your team *can* change that score, in your favor. After all, if every team that was favored to win always won, there would never be a need to play a game!

Earlier, in the section on penalty kicks, we talked about visualization (creating a mental image of where you want the ball to go, then actually "seeing" it hit that spot). Visualization works for the entire game of soccer. Many of the greatest athletes in the world use visualization to prepare for their games. Here's how you can, too.

A few hours before a game, start imagining what is going to happen. Use as much of your imagination as you can. Picture yourself—in your uniform, with your number— running onto the field for the start of the match. Watch yourself as you look at your teammates' faces, then at your opponents. Hear the opening whistle. Feel the grass as you run up the field. Listen to the sound of the ball as it's kicked, headed, and saved. You can even smell the grass!

Now, get more specific. Zero in on yourself. Imagine what will happen as the ball is kicked to you. If you're a striker, play a typical scene in your mind's eye: A teammate wins the ball. You move to support, then call "Man on!" You receive a pass with your foot, push it across your body to the other side, dribble twice, then make a mistake—the ball rolls away from you! But you recover quickly, and immediately win it back with a strong, well-timed tackle. You hear the coach yell "That's the way to stick in there!" A second later you hear your mom's voice: "Way to go, hon!"

Now you dribble upfield, with only the goalie to beat. You look up, see that the far post is open, and calmly fire a shot. You actually sense what it's like when your shoe hits the ball. You follow up strongly, with a little hop that adds extra power to the ball. You watch the ball all the way into the net—you actually see it push the red netting back. Finally, you hear the roar of the crowd, and feel the surge of excitement as your best friend races over and gives you a huge high five.

Whew!

Visualization works for everyone. If you're a defender, you can visualize what it's like to race back, arriving just in time to leap high and knock a header way wide, out of danger. If you're a keeper you can visualize watching an attack develop, getting your body low, glancing from side to side, getting screened, moving a couple of steps to see the ball again, tensing as the ball is struck, then springing to one side. It's a great feeling to make a save. You can actually feel the ball as it spins off your glove and out to the side where a fullback picks it up on the run and moves forward, into the attack.

Visualization takes a lot of imagination. But if you've played soccer long enough, you know exactly what a game is like. You smell the smells, hear the voices and shouts, feel the contact of soccer balls and bodies and . . . well, we don't have to tell you everything. Soccer is *your* game. So visualize as much as you can.

And then go out and play exactly the same way.

Unfortunately, visualization is not foolproof. Teams do lose. Sometimes you may be beaten by a better team; sometimes you may be beaten by a worse one.

That's life. But you know what? There's always another game.

Even if the season is over, there's another game next year. Sure you're upset. That's allowed. But what's not allowed is blaming yourself.

Let's say the worst possible thing happened: You missed an open goal in the final seconds. You shanked a penalty kick. You let the ball go through your fingers in goal.

Sure, you made a mistake. But you were not the only one.

Soccer is a game of mistakes. Soccer players make mistakes every second. The open goal you missed—what about all those other players who never even got close enough to shoot? The p.k. you muffed—what about all those other players who didn't want the pressure of taking it? The ball that went through your fingers—what about the six defensive errors that allowed the shot to be taken in the first place?

No one wants you to point fingers, and blame other people when you make a mistake. But you have to remember: Soccer is a team game. You win as a team, and you lose as a team. No one is solely responsible for a win, or a loss. You need your teammates to get you the ball, the same way you help feed them. You need your teammates to help defend, the same way you help them out on defense. You share everything together—victories; defeats; and those least satisfying of all results, ties.

The last part of mental preparation consists of one word: Enjoy.

Soccer is many things, but most of all it is fun. If you enjoy every second you are on the field, whether it is stretching, practicing, or playing a game, then you have found the key to mental preparation.

So enough talk. Go outside. Run. Kick. Dribble. Pass. Shoot. Defend. Save. And enjoy!

16 Watch and Learn

It's fun to have friends and family come to your games. Most people usually play better when they know they've got fans. (If you're one of those who gets nervous, don't worry. You're not alone!)

But soccer players are not always performers. Sometimes it's a player's turn to watch. One way to become a better player than you already are is to look at athletes who are already performing at a higher level: older players. The more high school, club, college, and pro games you see, the more you'll learn.

Fortunately, you've got plenty of games available nowadays. Soccer is played nearly year-round in most places, and the TV schedule is filled with matches. Find a few that sound interesting, and start watching.

But to become *really* good, you need to do more than just stare at the field or screen. Just as you must learn the correct way to shoot or pass, you need to learn to be an active, involved soccer viewer.

Here's how.

☻ Study players' techniques. As a high ball comes out of the air, watch the player who is about to receive it. See how quickly he decides which part of the body to use, how he positions his hands for balance, and what he does about opponents who are trying to get good position themselves. You can use this method for any kind of technique, from dribbling and shooting to tackling and goalkeeping. But don't overdo it. Concentrate on only one or two skills during a match (for example, making long passes and heading). And when you watch them being demonstrated, try to block everything else from your mind.

☻ Study only one player throughout a match. Select someone who plays the same position as you. Watch that player every time he or she touches (or does not touch) the ball. See if you can figure out his or her strengths and weaknesses. Is the player magic with the left foot, but will never use the right? Does he or she head well if there is no one around, but seldom go up in a crowd? Does the player rest for a couple of seconds whenever given the opportunity, or race around the field from end to end, then run out of gas before the end of the first half?

☻ Tactics are as important as technique. The key to watching tactics is to *not* keep your eye on the ball. In fact, study everything else *but* the ball. Choose a spot on the field far away from the action. Watch a player on the attacking team lull his defender into a false sense of security, then suddenly sprint into open space. Check out a defensive midfielder as he marks his man, then races into the penalty area to cover up a teammate's mistake. Ask yourself, "How did those players figure out what was going to happen before it did?" Then see if you can predict a similar situation *before* it happens.

⚽ Try to analyze team strategy, too. Make a game out of figuring out what formation each team uses (how many defenders, midfielders, and forwards they have). Check from time to time throughout the match to see if anything has changed—and how it has affected the flow of the game. Watch as both sides set up for and react to set plays (free kicks, corner kicks, goal kicks). If one team is down by a goal late in the game, try to figure out whether they're doing anything differently in an attempt to score. You may not always know the answers—but the more you think about the game off the field, the more likely you will be to come up with the right answers *on* it.

⚽ Try to get a feel for the "pace" of a game. Every match is played at a different tempo (speed). Some are frantic from start to finish; others are as slow paced as turtles in the sun. Sometimes every player seems to be doing something; other times only two or three appear to be moving. Many times, too, the pace changes *during* a game. See if you can understand why the tempo changes—then try to guess when it will shift next.

⚽ Use all the TV tools at your disposal. If you're watching on the tube, take advantage of whatever camera angle is being shown. If it's a long shot, look at where the attackers and defenders are positioned. Are they spread out or congested? Is that good or bad? If the camera shows a closeup, look closely at the view. How exactly is that guy dribbling, passing, or shooting? When instant replays are shown, examine them as if you were preparing for a test. Each time the same play is shown, watch a different player. Figure out what went right, and what went wrong. Ask yourself what you would have done in a similar situation. And don't forget to listen to the announcers as they describe formations, point out problems, and predict what will happen next. You can even pretend to talk with them. Think of questions you'd like to ask, or comments you'd like to make. If you do all these things, you'll wind up nearly as involved as the players themselves.

17 **Staying Healthy**

Soccer is a very safe sport—but it is a sport, and from time to time injuries and ailments are inevitable. You can help prevent problems by being as fit as possible (and of course wearing shin guards), but you can never be 100 percent sure nothing will happen.

Here are some common complaints (as well as suggestions about how to manage them!).

- ⚽ **Stitch.** This is a sharp pain in the stomach. It usually occurs when you've run a lot. The best way to get rid of a stitch is to breathe deeply through both your nose and mouth. You also might want to rest for a while.
- ⚽ **Cramps.** Muscle cramps affect muscles, usually in the calves and hamstrings. They can be caused by excessive fatigue, hunger and thirst, or dehydration. They also can

occur if you have not warmed up properly. If you get a cramp, stop what you are doing immediately (that won't be hard!), and stretch the muscle to relax the spasm. A good stretch for calves or hamstrings is to sit down, extend the leg as far forward as possible, then lean forward to touch your toes with your fingertips.

⊙ **Blisters.** These also seem minor, but they can really be a pain in the . . . foot. Most soccer players get blisters at some point; they often come from the friction of new shoes. You can reduce the likelihood of this happening by wearing new shoes around the house or yard for a couple of days before playing in them. You can also use foot powder, wear two pairs of socks, or rub Vaseline on the outside of the sock at the spot where friction usually occurs. If you do get a blister, *don't* pop it! Infection may result. Instead, cover it with a doughnut-shaped pad, and let it heal on its own. If it does happen to pop, clean it well and cover it with a bandage.

⊙ **Raspberries and strawberries.** These are not fruits; they're painful raw scrapes that come from falling and slide tackling. (They're red, which is why they're not called blueberries or blackberries.) When you start developing one, wash it well, then apply antibiotic ointment or powder. During practice and games, cover it with a gauze pad, and wrap it with a bandage. However, remove the cover when you're not playing; exposing it to the air helps it heal.

⊙ **Athlete's foot.** This is an annoying, itchy rash between your toes. Fortunately, antifungal powders and creams can clean up this infection quickly. You can lessen the chances of getting athlete's foot by always wearing slippers in the shower, and not trading shoes and socks with your teammates.

⚽ **Calluses.** These are masses of dead tissue (sounds nasty), sometimes filled with blood (even nastier). You can minimize the discomfort by taping a doughnut-shaped pad around it.

⚽ **Ingrown toenail.** Soak your toe in warm water for 15–20 minutes, three times a day. You can also place a gauze pad under the edge of the nail, lifting it away from the skin. Drugstores carry medications that help soften the nail, too.

⚽ **Shin splints.** These are a real pain—right in the shins, where you do so much running and kicking. You'll feel nagging pain and tenderness, usually at the start of a new season (because you haven't run or kicked for a while). Shin splints can also be caused by playing on a hard surface, wearing shoes with poor support, or running awkwardly. The best cure for shin splints is rest, ice, and aspirin. (Ice should be applied for 15–20 minutes at a time, with 15–20 minutes without ice in between. Do *not* apply heat to shin splints!) You can also try toe raises (standing on the ground, then slowly raising and lowering the heels). When you feel better and begin playing again, stretch your calves well before practices and games; also avoid jumping as much as possible. If you find yourself getting shin splints often, try changing to a soccer shoe with better padding, or one with more cleats.

⚽ **Ankle sprains.** With so much running in soccer, chances are at some point you may turn your ankle on a rough spot on the field, or during contact with another player. As with shin splints, and all other sprains and strains, the best treatment is RICE: Rest, Ice, Compression (wrapping the ice in an elastic bandage and pressing it against the injury), and Elevation (raising the ankle).

Especially in the first days after an injury such as this, do *not* apply heat (a heating pad or ointment like Ben-Gay)! This draws blood to the area, and actually slows the healing process.

⚽ **Pulls and strains.** Soccer players tend to pull their hamstring (the muscle in the back of the thigh) and groin (the muscle just below the abdomen) more than other muscles. If you feel tightness or a pain in these areas, rest is the most effective treatment. Good stretching before and after practice and games can strengthen these muscles, and reduce pulls and strains.

⚽ **Knee pain.** This can be caused by twisting the leg, knocking into another player, having weak quadricep (upper thigh) muscles, or simply growing quickly. Girls tend to get more knee injuries than boys, because of the way their bones and ligaments are formed. If you have persistent knee pain, see a sports doctor or orthopedist. He or she can prescribe strength exercises, and perhaps special orthotics (inserts) for your soccer shoes. To help prevent knee injuries by strengthening your quadriceps (and calves and ankles), do isometrics (pushing those muscles against immovable objects), leg raises, toe raises, and crunches. Swimming and bicycling also help strengthen weak knees.

⚽ **Nosebleeds.** This is fairly common. Put a small bag of ice on the bridge of your nose. Don't lean back! Then roll some gauze to plug your nostril. It looks kind of funny— but then again, this is soccer, not a fashion show!

⚽ **Asthma.** If you have asthma, you know that medication helps. Be sure to take it 20 minutes before training or games. If you use an inhaler, keep it in a warm spot (like a coach's or parent's pocket). Do not leave it in your soccer bag. You should also drink plenty of water before, during, and after soccer activity. Moisture helps keep your airways open.

⚽ **Sunburn.** This is troublesome, because it can lead to skin problems later on in life. Wear sunscreen as much as possible!

⚽ **General care of the feet.** A soccer player's most important asset is the . . . head. We assume you already know how to use your brain. However, your feet are also important. If you have any kind of foot ailment, whether it's a rash, blisters, or an ingrown toenail, you probably will not be able to dribble, pass, and shoot as well as you should. In addition, you will walk and run strangely—even off the field—which may lead to other problems. To avoid problems before they occur, wash your feet with soap and water after every practice or game. Dry them well before putting on your socks and shoes. (Wear clean socks every day!) Be aware of friction areas as soon as you feel a rubbing sensation, and take the actions above to prevent and treat blisters. Cut your toenails straight across—and cut them often. Be sure to wear shoes that fit properly, no matter what activity you are doing.

18 **Nutrition**

"You are what you eat." You may never have heard that weird expression, but it's certainly true for soccer players. If you eat the right foods, at the right time, you'll optimize all the hard work you're putting in on the field. If you eat the wrong stuff, or eat at the wrong time, much of that hard work will go to waste.

A soccer player is like a sports car. What good is having the nicest, coolest car in your neighborhood if you don't put high-performance gas in it? Even the most well-cared for car sputters and stalls if there's a ton of sugar and salt in the gas tank. See what we're getting at?!

If you want to perform at your peak, you should start with good nutrition the night *before* your game. Believe it or not, this is one of the most important meals you will eat. A healthy high-carbohydrate meal could include pasta with marinara sauce, baked potatoes with low-fat cheese and vegetables, small amounts of meat, rice, breads, fruits, ice milk, or sherbet.

The morning of your match, don't forget breakfast. Cereals are good (as long as they're not too high in fiber). So are bananas, apples, oatmeal, bread, toast, rolls, bagels, and boiled or poached eggs. For a drink, try orange juice.

Lunch (and dinner, if it's a late match) the day of a game can include lean chicken, pasta, peanut butter, cooked vegetables, cottage cheese, rice, potatoes (baked is best), low-fat yogurt, fresh, cooked, or dried fruit, pancakes, waffles, bagels, muffins, or toast and jelly. (Just eat *some* of these, not all—☺!) For drinks, go with fruit juice or milk. You should avoid sodas because they contain a lot of processed sugar and caffeine.

If you're going to play in a game, you should eat three to four hours before kickoff. (If that's impossible, try for a "liquid meal" like soup. It's easy to digest, which means you'll find it easier to run and pass, even think.)

There are a few foods to *definitely avoid* before a game. Some of them might be your favorites, but you can always eat them the next day: hamburger, sausage, steak, fried chicken, doughnuts, french fries, rich sauces and dressings like mayonnaise, and high-fiber salads. Stay away from sweet or concentrated drinks, too. And forget spicy foods—they make you too thirsty.

There is of course one drink that never fails: Water. It sounds plain and simple, but drinking plenty of water keeps your car—er, body—running at peak efficiency. Drinking lots of water 30 minutes before a game or practice, and whenever possible during a match or practice, keeps you from overheating. Water also transports energy, vitamins, and minerals throughout your body, giving you that extra boost you need to boot the ball strongly and accurately. Having your own water bottle allows you to drink as much as you can. (Of course, you've got to keep it filled!)

Good nutrition does not end when the final whistle blows. Eating poorly after games and workouts can make you tired. Eating too much protein (particularly meat, poultry, seafood, dairy products, and beans); or too many snacks like cookies and potato chips; or too much greasy, fatty food prevents your body from recovering as quickly as it could.

So what should you eat after a game or practice? Pasta, rice, bagels, pancakes, fruits, vegetables, juices, bananas, raisins, potatoes—and, of course, plenty of water.

It might not sound like the diet you're used to. But it is definitely the diet of champions!

19 Soccer Shoes (Don't Call Them "Cleats"!)

The right soccer shoes have never won a game. The wrong ones, however, have lost plenty.

If your feet hurt; if you've got blisters; if you can't run because your shoes are too tight—then you will not be as good a soccer player as you're training to be. That's why proper footwear is so important.

That does not necessarily mean you've got to have the most expensive kangaroo leather. Or the shoes with the fanciest logo, or latest technological design.

But it does mean you should have soccer shoes that fit; that won't fall apart the first time you play in rain or mud; and that allow you to kick, run, and jump without ever thinking about your feet.

When you buy soccer shoes, bring a parent or other adult along. He or she can help determine if a particular shoe (actually, both of them—you should always buy both a left *and* right!) is good for you. Ultimately, however, you're the player who will be wearing them, so you should think about certain shoe-related things. For example:

⚽ What's on the bottom? "Studs," or "cleats"—the round things that connect the shoe to the ground—are crucial.

(Try not to refer to the entire shoe as "cleats." That's like calling your mom a "house" just because she lives in one. Uh-oh. We didn't say that.) The pattern, height, and size of the cleats determines how much support the shoe will give your ankle and foot, as well as how easily you'll be able to move on different types of surfaces. Most players should start out with molded cleats (these are rubber, and there are lots of them). Because young players need good support, you should not get screw-in cleats (metal— they're longer, and there are fewer of them) until you're older. (Screw-ins are also good for wet surfaces, or fields with high grass. Older players usually have both moldeds and screw-ins, and decide which they will wear based on field conditions.)

⚽ Try on as many different shoes as you can stand, before deciding on one. Make sure you're wearing soccer socks. Stand up; see if your toes feel snug against the front of the shoe. Then put all your weight on each foot. If the shoe does not spread out enough to support your entire weight, don't buy it. Now try juggling a soccer ball, to see how comfortable the shoe feels. Finally, jog a few steps. No shoe will feel perfect the first time (they will stretch a bit to fit your foot); however, you should never buy a shoe that actually *hurts*.

⚽ Your mom or dad might ask about buying a shoe that is a bit big, because you'll grow into it. This doesn't work for soccer. You won't be able to "feel" the ball when you kick it, and you won't be able to run very well either. Wearing three pairs of socks won't help. If you're growing fast, and cost is an issue, see if your club has a program where parents can trade or exchange shoes (and other equipment) as players get older.

⚽ It is important to break in your shoes. The first time you wear them should not be during a game. Instead, soak your new shoes in lukewarm water. Then put them on (yeah, we know it sounds and looks funny), and walk around the house. As the shoes dry, they will mold to the same shape as your foot. Even then, you should wear them to a couple of practices before using them in a game. To help keep the shape you want, use a shoe tree, or stuff them with newspaper (make sure your parents are not in the middle of reading it at the time!).

⚽ Don't throw dirty soccer shoes in a washing machine! It sounds simple, but it's not smart. Instead, use mild soap and cold water to get rid of mud and dirt. To dry, put them *away* from a direct heat source, like a radiator. (It goes without saying that the microwave is out!) After your shoes have dried, use leather conditioner, polish, or saddle soap to help keep the leather fresh. You should get in the habit of polishing your shoes often. You can buy special polish the same place you buy soccer shoes.

⚽ Lacing is important. The "unlaced" look might be cool for school and the mall, but it definitely does not work on the soccer field. Try to keep your laces on the outside of the shoe, so they don't interfere with your kicking. Don't lace them up over your socks—it's dangerous. And if your laces are too long, get shorter ones!

20 It's in the Bag

One of your most important soccer possessions will never make it onto the field. Without it, however, you yourself may never get on the field.

We're talking, of course, about your soccer bag. It's amazing how much stuff you can stuff into a good, sturdy one. (It's also amazing what happens if you don't air it out every so often!)

A good soccer bag contains the following:

- ⚽ **Uniform:** Shirt, shorts, socks, shoes (does everything in *s*occer start with *s*?!) If you don't wear your uniform to your game, it's a good idea to pack it all the night before. If you've got a couple of jerseys or pairs of shoes, throw them in, too. You never know when they might come in handy.
- ⚽ **Shin guards.** Many coaches and referees will not let you on the field without them. (In some leagues and tournaments, shin guards are *mandatory*—you must have them). It doesn't hurt to carry a couple of extra pairs, for teammates who forget theirs.
- ⚽ **Ball.** Be sure your name and phone number are on it— in indelible ink. Bring a small ball pump, too.

☉ **Warm-ups.** No matter how hot it seems, soccer fields have a way of turning cool.

☉ **Athletic tape.** Tape can be used for everything, from holding up your socks to keeping your shoes together if they suddenly fall apart. Oh yes, it also can be used for the reason it was invented: to secure bandages.

☉ **Food!** Snacks (trail mix, fresh fruit, and dried fruit such as apricots and raisins) are great; so are bagels. Ditto for water or fruit juice boxes. Stay away from food that might make a mess if, let's say, someone sits on your bag by mistake.

☉ **Sunscreen.** Use it! It helps prevent sunburn today, and skin problems when you get older.

Index